SCENES FROM THE PAST :
EAST LANCASHIRE I
- BURY -
to HEYWOOD and RAWTENSTALL

From the Heywood Station footbridge, looking west, we have a glimpse of the town's streets as they were in the 1960s. A Newton Heath shed Black 5 draws away from the "Bury" platform with train number 1T50, the 10.10 Todmorden to Llandudno service, with nine carriages in tow. This was a Saturday morning train, captured on film as it leaves the station at 10.32 on the 10th July 1965. Bridge No 3 carries Manchester Street, one of the principal thoroughfares in the town, and upon which the appropriately-named "Railway Inn" overlooks the station. Note the extant gas lamp standards, probably no longer in use, and the reverse side of a banner signal mounted on the Down platform. Banner signals were positioned in order to aid footplate crews as to the disposition of the next signals which, in this case, were out of sight at Green Lane crossing. Of interest are the motor vehicles: a Seddon lorry awaits an exit from Cowburn Street, as a Rover 12 glides past. A rather smart Austin A60 has been parked at the end of Railway Street. Those readers with a penchant for carriage torpedo ventilators have a few here to study.
Eric Bentley

JEFFREY WELLS & ERIC BENTLEY

Copyright © E F Bentley, J Wells, Foxline.

ISBN 1 870119 56 8

All rights reserved

Printed by the Amadeus Press, Huddersfield.

Published by Foxline, 32 Urwick Road,
Romiley, Stockport. SK6 3JS

Bury Bolton Street. The views below illustrate what could almost be described as "timeless", insofar as the many thousands of visitors who these days visit the East Lancashire Railway will find them instantly recognisable, despite the fact that the most recent, by Eric Bentley, was photographed as long ago as 1965. British Railways were custodians at the time when both scenes were recorded, the upper, showing a pair of Stanier Class 5's (train engine No **45348** - 6G, Llandudno Jcn) working the 09.50 (1C65) Llandudno-Manchester Victoria, extended to Rams-bottom, entering the smoky confines of the short tunnel beneath Bolton Street (Saturday 10th july 1965). The lower, enlarged view, dates from 1953 following completion of the new entrance from Bolton Street.

Publishers Note: During the preparation of this book, Eric Bentley sadly became terminally ill. Along with Jeffrey Wells, I was able to, in the comparatively short time I had known the Bentleys, enjoy the company of both Eric and his wife Jean. Eric continued to be enthusiastic about the project despite his failing health, but with most of the written work complete, he gained some satisfaction in seeing a large part of the book in proof form. Throughout what has been a difficult period, Jean has been ever supportive. I offer most sincerely my thanks for that continued help and the opportunity to publish Eric's fine work. *Greg Fox.*

Acknowledgements: Right up to the time of Eric's untimely passing, it was clear that both authors had obtained a great deal of pleasure from the preparation of this work. It was recognised that without the interest and help of a number of people the task of compiling such a wealth of pictorial content would not have been possible. It is fitting to extend our gratitude to the kindness of Fred Collinge, Peter Duncan, Ray Farrell, David Hampson, Ian G Holt, Eddie Johnson, Jim Peden, Bill Reid, Brian Stephenson (RAS), Allan Sommerfield, Stuart Taylor and not least to Greg Fox for his inspiration. Thanks are also due to the reference libraries at Bury and Rawtenstall, to the LYR Society for its permission to reproduce from its photograph collection, and to Andrew Coward.

Jeffrey Wells, Greenfield. February 2000.

Bury Bolton Street seen here shortly after the reconstruction of 1951-52. These new station buildings at road level replaced rather ornate but life expired structures dating from 1883. Following provision of the new bus/rail Interchange in 1980, the station here was subsequently acquired by the East Lancashire Light Railway Company. The station is seen here decorated for the Queen Elizabeth II Coronation celebrations of 1953.

Prologue

In its railway heyday, the small town of Bury could claim to have its fair share of railway features. There were two railway stations, a steam motive power depot, an electric car depot, ten signal boxes (within an area bounded by Gigg Mill, Loco Jct, Bury Gas Works, and Tottington Jct), two goods stations, and ample siding accommodation. The bulk of these were located on the western side of the town, on the left bank of the River Irwell, and were clustered about the cross-roads formed by the intersection of the south to north, and east to west routes. The map on the inside of the front cover shows the arrangement of Bury's railway infrastructure at the latter end of the heyday - in 1950.

The Origins of Bury's Railways

On the 14th September 1843, a meeting was held at which it was decided to promote a railway from Clifton, near Manchester, along the valley of the Irwell, via Bury and Ramsbottom, to Rawtenstall. The Company formed to undertake this assumed the name of "The Manchester, Bury and Rossendale Railway", the formal incorporation of which occurred on the 4th July 1844. While the railway was under construction this Comany amalgamated with another, the "Blackburn, Bury, Accrington and Colne Extension Railway", whereupon the Manchester, Bury and Rossendale changed its name to the more familiar "East Lancashire Railway". This was accomplished on the 21st July 1845, and

with this amalgamation came a change of purpose, for now the real determination was to extend the line to Accrington, leaving the line to Rawtenstall in second place in the order of things.

The ELR's line between Clifton Junction and Rawtenstall was inspected on the 23rd September 1846; this was a double line as far as Stubbins, then single to Rawtenstall. Formal opening took place on the 25th September 1846. The first train to run from Clifton Junction to Rawtenstall commenced its journey in Manchester and conveyed invited guests and town officials. This ran in an atmosphere of jubilation, a crowd of 600 passengers alighting at Rawtenstall to enjoy "an elegant collation" within the new weaving shed belonging to John Robinson Kay. With this new line of railway, Bury found itself, at last, connected to the outside world, following years of isolation in an economic climate which demanded ever faster communication. Public services began three days later on the 28th.

Influential people were also intent on proposing a railway which would connect Liverpool, Lancashire's chief port, with the industrial hinterland which embraced Wigan, Bolton, Bury, and Rochdale, and even beyond to the West Riding of Yorkshire. By an Act dated 27th July 1846, the "Liverpool and Bury Railway" was initiated, but even while construction of the line was underway, the powerful Manchester and Leeds Railway absorbed the Liverpool and Bury with effect from the 1st October 1846. The

Ancient and modern at the south end of Bolton Street Station, 24th February 1954. This LM Region Publicity Department view of the station name signscomplements the ornate iron work of Tenterden Street bridge.
BR(LMR)

MLR had already constructed a branch line between Blue Pits (Castleton) and Heywood, opening it for traffic on the 15th April 1841 (without the consent of Parliament). The MLR changed its identity to the Lancashire and Yorkshire Railway on the 9th July 1847, the same Act authorising the Liverpool and Bury line to continue to Heywood to form an end-on connection with the Heywood Branch. Thus by the 20th November 1848, a route between the Yorkshire towns and Liverpool had been forged which provided a much needed alternative route to the Liverpool and Manchester Railway. The ELR which had done so much in establishing a network of railways in Lancashire, was itself absorbed by the LYR on the 13th August 1859.

The two main routes intersected in Bury but apart from an east to north curve known as the "Bury East Fork" which had been authorised by the above-mentioned 9th July Act, the two railways were not allowed to cross each other on the level, or to form a more complex junction. This explains why the east to west route dipped beneath the ELR line west of Knowsley Street station in what the LYR records refer to as "The Hollow".

The Extension Line

The section of railway between Stubbins Junction and Accrington (7¼ miles) was opened for traffic on the 17th August 1848. Overshadowed by its larger neighbour to the south, Stubbins station could claim the credit of being the location of the actual junction between the Extension Line to Accrington, and the secondary line to Rawtenstall. Passenger trains on the main line passed through Stubbins non-stop: there were no platforms serving

the main line. Instead, the station catered for the local stopping trains heading to and coming from Rawtenstall and Bacup.

The contractor for the Extension Line was John Brogden who, having had his tender of £105,000 accepted, found his work cut out for him. The line left Stubbins Junction (just to the south of the station) and maintained an almost parallel course to the Rawtenstall line, climbing all the while, and passing firstly over Alderbottom Viaduct (valley of the Irwell), and then the nine stone arches of Lumb Viaduct (over the Irwell again). From here, the line swung north westwards, over the Ogden Viaduct (the Ogden valley) and onwards to Helmshore station. These were all heavy construction works which the contractor had to undertake. Even beyond Helmshore, a viaduct of fourteen arches had to be constructed to be constructed a viaduct of 14 arches to carry the railway over the River Ogden and Helmshore Mills Reservoir, along with massive retaining walls.

The ruling gradients between Stubbins and Helmshore were 1 in 73 and 1 in 85 rising: footplate crews also had a hard task until the summit of the line was reached (771 feet above sea level), five miles from Stubbins. Coming the other way from Accrington was equally hard. The 1 in 40 gradient out of the town required the assistance of banking engines on most trains. Helmshore station, 6 miles from Bury, was opened on the 17th April 1848. Before alterations took place by the LYR in the 1880s, the station bore the hallmarks of the John Shae Perring's design. (J S Perring, the Company's chief engineer). The Up platform possessed the main station buildings with the booking office conveniently positioned adjacent to the level crossing formed by the Haslingden to Helmshore road. Half way along the same platform was the

Helmshore, January 1960. With one of the last steam hauled workings prior to replacement by Dmu's, **42661**, a long time Accrington based engine, rolls into Helmshore with an Accrington to Manchester Victoria train. Of particular interest is the cattle dock which had only recently received new gates, fencing and walls. Goods facilities were to be withdrawn from the 7th September 1964, such was the rapid nature of change on the railways. Helmshore enjoys a special place in the annals of present day East Lancashire Railway Company history, being arguably the "birthplace" of the organisation. *courtesy T Sherratt*

small ELR goods warehouse, a timber structure mounted on a brick base. In many respects, the layout of the station, with its footbridge and signal box lying on either side of the level crossing, was a mirror-image of the larger station at Ramsbottom. Helmshore station closed on the 5th December 1966.

Helmshore has a special place in the evolution of the East Lancashire Railway Preservation Society. In October 1966, the Helmshore and District Railway Preservation Society was formed out of a group of enthusiasts, only to be disbanded without much achieved on the 9th April 1968. In the following June, the ELRPS found its feet, this being a hybrid of the earlier Helmshore-based society. On the 16th August 1969 the first ELRPS museum opened at Helmshore station, and in January 1971, the East Lancashire Light Railway Co. Ltd emerged as an offshoot of the ELPRS, its aim being to buy the Haslingden Grane Road to Stubbins Junction line. The rails at Helmshore, however, were removed by the BRB in October 1971 and the focus of preservation shifted to Bury, the opening of the Bury Transport Museum being the manifestation of the ELRPS' determination and hard work.

Bury's Passenger and Goods Stations

The ELR Company decided to concentrate its operations at Bury. The first permanent station opened as Bury E L on the 28th September 1846 with the Company's imposing administration offices built alongside. The station, offices, and the adjacent yard were confined within a cutting flanked by high retaining walls on both sides (except for a short bank on the Down side), some 20 to 25 feet high. The station continued to function in its original form until rebuilt by the LYR in the 1880s. By then it had received its

now familiar name of Bolton Street (as from February 1866). The rebuilt station was completed in the summer of 1883 at a cost of between £10,000 and £12,000, and involved the raising and lengthening of the platforms, removing the ELR train shed roof and replacing it with canopies over each platform. Most of the station amenities (waiting rooms, wcs, staff quarters, offices, etc) were located on the Up (Manchester) platform.

Further modifications to the station were made by the LYR in preparation for the Manchester to Bury electric trains in 1916, and such innovation was to continue; bi-directional signalling was installed on platform lines 3 and 4 by the 1st September 1918. Bolton Street became a closed station, meaning that without a ticket, admission to the platforms was prohibited past a set of barriers manned, during the Great War, by female ticket collectors.

The station that we know today owes its character as much to the major changes which took place by British Railways following a fire which destroyed the station booking hall (with its turret clock) and footbridge on the 14th May 1947. The new station frontage on Bolton Street, and the footbridge and stairs leading from it were opened on the 30th June 1952.

The ELR headquarters faced on to platform 2 (the Up platform). The building was a three-storey block which was characterised by stone quoins, arched windows and doorways: a solid monument of brick, graced with a shallow hipped roof of slate through which projected brick chimney stacks; an altogether Dickensian edifice. Instead of being kept as a memorial to the ELR, the building was demolished between October 1973 and June 1974, the void left behind now filled by the East Lancashire Railway's restaurant.

This First World War period view illustrates well the station buildings that fronted Bolton Street until the the fire of 1947, which virtually destroyed the booking hall and connecting footways to the platforms. Part of the station in this 1915 scene was being used for army recruitment, hence the appropriate signs. Those not having any military responsibilities however, could be attracted by the "Tourist tickets" on offer, or even a trip to Southport.   *NRM*

An area of the station not seen by the general public lies beneath the existing 1952 booking hall and adjacent offices. Built by the ELR as part of the original station is a series of connecting vaults with stone walls and arched, brick ceilings. Unknowingly, the motorist and pedestrian passes over these "catacombs" as he moves along the sloping approach to and from the car park. The cellars are now mostly unlit and dank, but afford storage accommodation for the ELR Company.

Bury's second station occupied a low-level site next to the bridge carrying Knowsley Street out of the town centre. The station was opened by the LYR on the 1st May 1848 as Bury Low Level, the name "Market Place" awarded to the station between February 1866 until sometime in 1888 when it assumed the name of Knowsley Street. The amenity grew in size by gradual accretion, buildings being added in a piecemeal and apparently haphazard fashion. By 1891, alterations took place in order to accommodate four lines of way through the station, both platforms served by a line each, and two through roads in the middle. Further improvements occurred in 1896/7. LYR Board Minutes, dated 22nd April 1896, indicate that the tender of C Brierley, (£1,912.10.1), had been accepted for the alterations to a platform roof, a new staircase, and the raising of the platforms (this being a legal requirement by the end of the 1880s). Additional platform roofing

was tendered for three years later, almost to the day. Knowsley Street station was always regarded as second best, located as it was at some distance from the heart of the town. Nevertheless, it was well-remembered by many on three counts: the unmistakable "Bury Hollow" where westbound trains dipped beneath the ELR line as they left the station, and eastward bound trains slogged their way for a short distance up the brow; the day the footbridge collapsed (19th January 1952) under the burden of 200 Blackburn Rovers football supporters awaiting their train home; and, on a happier note, the days of excursions and the early July holiday trains which carried thousands away for a week or two. Knowsley Street closed on the 5th October 1970, and was razed to the ground the following April.

Bury also handled goods at two goods stations and a variety of railway-owned and private sidings. In 1904, there were 18 sidings in the town serving the local industries; Bury Gas Siding was one of them, completed in 1893 under the auspices of the Corporation to facilitate the reception of coal for the retorts, and the distribution of coal tar and coke. By 1925, the number of sidings had declined to 15. Knowsley Street station covered the largest area devoted to goods traffic, situated west of the passenger station. The yard was dominated by a large brick warehouse (one of three - the other two were smaller) erected in 1912. The high

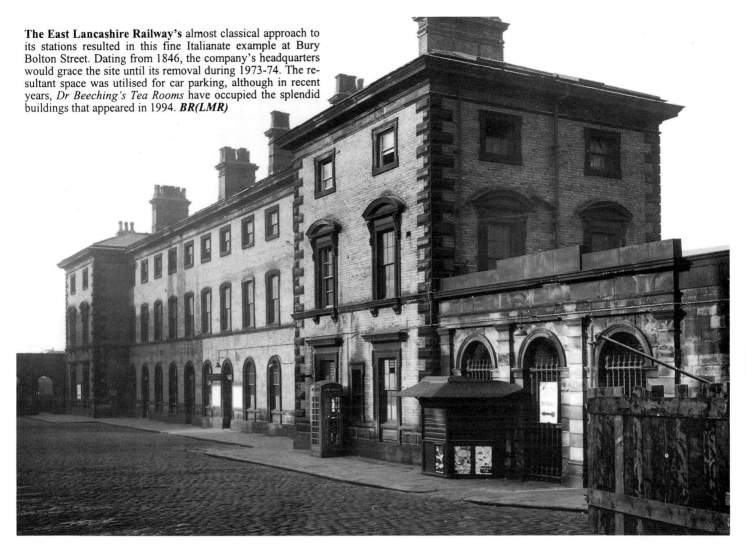

The East Lancashire Railway's almost classical approach to its stations resulted in this fine Italianate example at Bury Bolton Street. Dating from 1846, the company's headquarters would grace the site until its removal during 1973-74. The resultant space was utilised for car parking, although in recent years, *Dr Beeching's Tea Rooms* have occupied the splendid buildings that appeared in 1994. ***BR(LMR)***

wall of this warehouse backed the Down bay platform and formed an imposing reminder of earlier days - on the highest part of the wall was the bold lettering "Lancashire and Yorkshire Railway". Photographs taken in the mid 1960s show the goods sidings packed with covered vans - even then a hive of activity. The 1912 goods warehouse was demolished in 1971.

By contrast, Castlecroft goods yard, lying to the north of Bury EL Tunnel, was small. It suffered from being hemmed in by the main running lines and the surrounding streets. As early as 1848, the ELR had built a stone warehouse which was served by seven sidings, two of which ran inside. Despite its modest size, Castlecroft goods station handled much freight during LYR days and into the 1930s. It served many of Bury's manufacturers which were located nearby. On the 26th August 1972 the ELRPS opened the building as Bury Transport Museum.

Forks and Loops

As previously mentioned, Bury East Fork was an early provision by the ELR which allowed its trains from its line to run on to the east-west route, and vice versa. The Fork was opened on the 20th November 1848, and has been described by Eric Mason as "a steeply graded and curved connection"(1). Until it was closed to traffic, it served Bury for over 100 years, last of all as a single line

over which Yorkshire coal trains headed for the Rawtenstall Coal Concentration Plant, before returning with empties.

The Bury Loop was longer, less steeply graded, and of less curvature. It connected the east - west route at Bury Loop Junction with the Clifton to Accrington ELR line at Bury Loco Junction, south of Buckley Wells. Work began on the Loop in 1898 and involved a 70 yards long covered way beneath both Manchester Old and New Roads. The Loop was inspected by the Board of Trade and opened for traffic on the 11th July 1899. On the 27th March 1967, it was closed following a fire which had destroyed Bury Loop Junction signal box. Part of the Loop was, however, re-instated in 1980 when the Manchester - Bury electric service transferred from Bolton Street Station to the new Bury Interchange.

The Buckley Wells Area

As early as 1846 an ELR locomotive works existed in the form of wooden huts close to Coal Pit Lane. These were soon found to be inadequate, and a new locomotive repair shop was planned and finally built, after much delay, in the summer of 1856 to the design of J S Perring, at a cost of £6,600. Enlargement and alterations were carried out in the succeeding years by the LYR. The building, which was from the start a modular design and capable of extension, finally reached a length of nearly 600 feet. In this, locomotives were repaired and rebuilt, and between 1860 and 1862, sixteen locomotives were produced for the Company. **(2)**

In 1876 a new engine shed was constructed which could be approached on foot along Coal Pit Lane. The new shed lay to the east of the locomotive workshops, sharing a party-wall with it. In the 1930s the eight-road, brick straight shed had a standardised hipped roof profile, surmounted by rows of tall ventilators. The shed yard possessed a brick tank-over coal stage, a sand-drying plant, a 50ft diameter electrically operated turntable, and four water columns. The LYR designated the shed No.20; the LMS, C20; and BR (LMR), 26D, under the parent shed Newton Heath, 26A; and finally 9M as from September 1961. The shed ended its days as a locomotive storage depot, finally closing on the 12th April 1965, and was demolished in late November 1975.

The original ELR workshops had been readily converted to rolling stock maintenance and repair following the opening of the LYR workshops at Horwich in January 1888. Again, in 1916, the building was eminently suitable for conversion into an electric car depot, capable of handling the five-car sets of the Manchester - Bury electric stock. Thus it remained until closure in September 1991.

Three Focal Points

Ramsbottom. Lying four miles north of Bury in the Irwell valley, is the small industrial cum residential town of Ramsbottom. A station opened here on the 28th September 1846, conveniently placed next to the level crossing formed by Bridge Street crossing the railway. From the early days, the station served as a break-of-journey point for changing trains, depending on whether the traveller from Bury was to continue to Accrington or Rawtenstall, and finally Bacup. In the 1950s the stopping place had a spread of sidings on the east side of the station, a larger expanse of sidings (Ramsbottom Sidings) on the northern side and an ELR vintage goods warehouse (demolished in December 1968) at the end of the Down platform which was lined with a long brick wall and canopy to protect waiting travellers from the weather. In addition to the station goods facilities, there were a number of private sidings serving such notable concerns as Square Bleach Works and Ramsbottom Paper Mill. An LMS 1938 signal box stood on the Down side on the opposite side of the level crossing; this was closed after the passage of a Dmu special train on the 28th March 1982. The station closed on the 3rd June 1972 and was re-opened by the ELR Co., as the Phase 1 terminus on 25th July 1987 with the new stone built ELR style station building following on 19th June 1989. Ramsbottom signal box also took on a new lease of life on the 17th November 1990 to control, as it always had done, the level crossing, and progressively, the north and south end of the loop, and the north sidings, coming into full operation on the 27th April 1991 with the Phase 2 opening to Rawtenstall.

Rawtenstall. There seems to be some confusion about the architectural origin of Rawtenstall station. In some quarters it is believed that the design was by J S Perring who was responsible for many of the stations for the ELR; others hold that the station was to the design of Messrs Holden, architects, Manchester. According to the Manchester Guardian, 11th August 1849:

"Rawtenstall station has a very neat edifice, on the right for the station offices, waiting rooms, etc, which was designed by Messrs Holden, architects, Manchester, who also designed the central office of the company and station at Bury, all the other stations on the line being designed by Mr Perring, the company resident engineer.....".

This sounds straightforward until the same newspaper, 8th September 1849, recorded that,

"The principal station edifices are at Bury....... And Accrington, which is great junction station. Both these edifices are from designs by Messrs Holden, architects of Manchester. All other stations on the eastern line of the company, from Clifton to Colne and to Newchurch, on the Rossendale branch, are from a uniform and novel design by Mr John Shae Perring".

Only when we turn to Harrison and Sale's Guide to the ELR, dated 1849, can we be certain of the true identity of the designer. In a brief description, the Guide reveals that :-

"The Bury station is from a design by Messrs Holden, architects of Manchester. All other stations...... from Clifton to Colne, and to Newchurch on the Rossendale Branch are of an uniform and novel design by the company's resident engineer".

This accords with the second of the Guardian reports above.

Today, Rawtenstall is the terminus of the ELR Co's., line complete with a "modern" ELR pattern single-storey building familiar to the hosts of passengers who have plied the line to and from Bury. The original station, on opening, was served by a single line until July 1857, the single platform with its collection of amenities (booking office and station master's house) representing the town's railway focus until doubling of the line took place in 1857 established a second platform. The Down platform in LYR days possessed fewer facilities of timber construction and could be reached by a footbridge and the level crossing end of the station. The station had more to it than met the eye; below ground level on the Up side there were cellars used for storage. Even in LMS and BR days the Down platform sufficed with nothing more than timber waiting rooms and a measure of protection beneath a ridge and furrow awning of 1890s vintage. A three-storey goods warehouse, built circa 1858/9, stood for Rawtenstall's goods station, this being extended by the LYR by the addition of a lower building in the 1890s. The goods shed, cattle pens, and sidings were sandwiched between the passenger station, Bury Road, and New Hall Hey Road. The goods yard was utilised for the Coal Concentration Plant until December 1980. Rawtenstall station closed on the 5th June 1972, and re-opened on the 27th April 1991, the new stone station buildings being fully opened on the 16th April 1992.

Heywood. The earliest station at this typical Lancashire mill town dated back to the opening of the 1¾ mile MLR branch from Blue Pits (Castleton) on the 15th April 1841. According to

Knowsley Street station. Bury Corporation Tramways was inaugurated on 3 June 1903 during the heyday of urban tramway development. The last trams in the town ran until 13 February 1949. In this excellent view we see vehicle No.11 coming to a halt outside Knowsley Street station for people to alight. Following some distance behind is a Bury Corporation omnibus on route 8 and heading for the town centre. The date of the photograph is unknown but appears to have been taken in the early post-war years. No effort has been made to remove the large sign affixed to the station building - the formation of British Railways taking place with effect from 1 January 1948. Note that the surface of Knowsley Street is paved with "lonkies", the colloquial term for the thousands of stone blocks which form the metalled surface of many northern streets. Of interest too is the bold inscription along the wooden extension to the bridge parapet which proclaims the name of the station.   *W A Camwell*

Captain Tucker's survey in 1848, this station was a terminus train shed served by a single line whilst a small building (engine shed?) marked the very end of the branch. The station building was located about 88 yards to the north east of the Heywood Branch Canal in what became an area of goods sidings on the eastern side of the later station. This early station was short-lived, however, and closed on the 1st May 1848 to be replaced by a second station cap-able of accommodating through traffic between Castleton and Bury. The Manchester Guardian, ever cognisant of local goings on of importance, referred to the new station in its 3rd May 1848 issue:

> *"At present there is only a temporary erection as a station at Heywood, but a large and commodious one is intended to be erected on the site of the present building, which from its contiguity to the market on the south side of the town is exceedingly convenient".*

The new station was located on the outermost bend of the railway as it curved south through the southern flanks of the town centre, the actual site chosen being but a short distance north of the terminus of the canal. The curve was severe enough to preclude the passage of large locomotives such as the Royal Scot class which would have been unable to negotiate the station platforms. The station facilities were concentrated on the Up side (Rochdale platform), access to which could be made from the appropriately named "Railway Street" on the north side of the station.

Drab the town was with its sombre spinning mills and rows of terraced housing, and likewise the no-nonsense LYR station. This Company decided to refurbish the station in 1883:

the contractor, J H Nowell was awarded the contract on the 10th July of that year, to construct a new platform roof, waiting rooms and booking office. As if to off-set the drab surroundings, the contractor fitted a decorative valance to the periphery of the platform canopies. As one writer has commented, *"of all the different styles of valancing use by the Lancashire and Yorkshire Railway, this design is by far the most ornate".* **(3)** Heywood station closed to passengers on the 5th October 1970.

Postscript

The directors, engineers, contractors, Company servants, and many others would never have imagined the demise of the East Lancashire Railway. Although the Company was subsumed into the LYR in 1859, the name lived on, and continues to do so under the auspices of a Society which has resurrected not only the line between Bury and Rawtenstall, but also a section of the line of the erstwhile Liverpool and Bury Company, between Bury and Heywood. A few monuments remain of the two founding companies in the form of bridges and tunnels. On a recent visit to Bury, I was able to observe the ELR coat of arms *Celeritate et Utilitate* in the most unexpected place, on the southern end of Bury EL Tunnel carved in solid rock, weathered but visible, after close on 150 years. Not far away, stands the bridge carrying Manchester Road over the east - west railway, exhibiting a peculiar skewed masonry at both ends of the arch, and its neighbour carrying Knowsley Street, proclaiming still "1848". Monuments each to the first railways through the town. Today, Bury can boast that it is the headquarters of the only preserved railway in the country which passes over both a rapid transport system, the Metrolink, and a motorway, the M66.

(1) Eric Mason, *The Lancashire and Yorkshire Railway in the 20th Century, p.32.* The actual gradient, according to a BoT accident report of 1871 was as follows: from Bolton Street Station - 1 in 90 for 66 yards, then 1 in 59 for 154 yards, giving the distance of the Fork as 220 yards. The radius of the Fork has been calculated to be about 7 chains.

(2) Andrew Wilson, East Lancashire Railway, *Steam Days, May 1998.*

3) G H Foxley, *LYRS Journal No.18, p.9.*

EAST LANCASHIRE LINES
- BURY -
HEYWOOD & RAWTENSTALL
(and connecting lines)

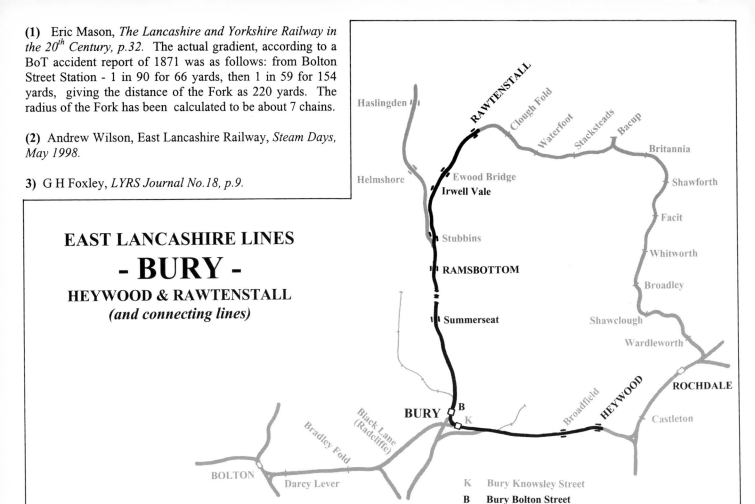

K Bury Knowsley Street
B Bury Bolton Street

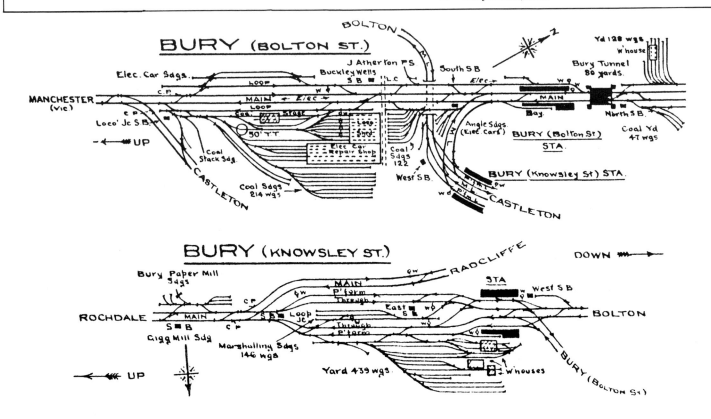

Bury to Heywood

Bury shed's own "Crab", 42700, leaves Knowsley Street Station with a Rochdale to Southport excursion at 11.50, Friday, 7th June 1963. Of interest is Bury West signal box, opened by the LYR in 1909 as box No.375, the squat multi-armed telegraph poles with its wooden circuit box, and the wooden channel leading to it, up and over the retaining wall. Affixed to the smokebox door of the Crab is the reporting number 1T65. These numbers were a common feature to be seen on excursion trains, and an essential aid to signalmen, station, and carriage sorting staff. In the days of numerous summer excursions, reporting numbers displayed on the front of the engine distinguished the special trains from the usual scheduled trains. The photograph has been taken from the footbridge which spanned the line north of Buckley Wells, the camera catching the relatively new Bury Town Hall, and the stop-block at the end of one of Angle Sidings. The East Fork is mostly hidden from view by vegetation, but coincides with the white concrete cabin to the left of the stop-block.

Eric Bentley

(Above) "Austerity" 90267 (Bolton) climbs towards Knowsley Street Station in the early afternoon of Tuesday, 26th February 1963, with a train of empty 16 ton mineral wagons on a Bolton to Royton Junction trip. Dominating the view is the Town Hall, whilst to its right is the booking office fronting the station. The tightly curved and steeply graded East Fork passed through the left-hand arch of Manchester Road Bridge (No.20) to join the main line. Bridge 20 had a main line span of 51feet 2ins, and a Fork line skew span of 33feet. The engine was a product of expediency in the Second World War, being built in 1943 by the North British Locomotive Company.   *Eric Bentley*

Local to Liverpool. The signal is off for a distinctly grimy Ivatt 4-6-0 2MT **46402** (Bank Hall) to take the Down Slow line out of Knowsley Street Station, at 08.59 precisely, Saturday, 10th July 1965. The run-of-the-mill local service was one of the many between Rochdale and the ex-LYR's Liverpool Exchange Station until it closed its doors to passengers on 30th April 1977. Apart from the fine study of the track work forming the junction, the reader's attention is drawn to the lattice signal post and the underslung boards mounted on a steel frame. Note the steel guy-rods supporting the right-hand bracket, the long ladder, and the smoke deflector. The other board applied to the Down Fast line. In June 1969, the signals relating to the Up and Down Fast lines operated from Bury West signal box were removed whilst connections between, to, and from the Fast lines were secured out of use pending removal. The remaining Down and Up Slow lines were renamed the Down and Up Main lines respectively. But that was four years into the future, and heralded the closure of the Rochdale to Bolton line completely.

Eric Bentley

On Saturday, 28th July 1962, the Roch Valley Railway Society ran a special tour (reporting number 1Z30) from Manchester London Road Station, via Oldham, Rochdale, Facit, Rochdale, Heap Bridge, Bury, Tottington, Bury, Bacup, Radcliffe, Bradley Fold Junction, Radcliffe, Prestwich, and finally returning to Manchester Victoria. At 16.00, the tour is seen leaving Knowsley Street Station on the Down Fast, and taking the East Fork to Bolton Street Station, the veteran ex-LYR 3F 0-6-0 **52523** travelling tender first. The small bevy of enthusiasts on the footplate will have no doubt appreciated the cramped space in which the crew had to work, and normally without the presence of four others! The magnificent arch carrying Knowsley Street over the junction had a span of 60 feet 2 ins; it was built in 1848, and built to last.

The full elevation of Knowsley Street bridge (No.19) casts a shadow over the actual junction of the Rochdale to Bolton line and the East Fork. A Stanier 2-6-4 4MT tank engine , **42550** of Bury shed, takes the single slip into Knowsley Street Station, while at the Down platform an unidentified "Black Five" awaits departure with the 15.40 Rochdale to Wigan Wallgate local service. Peeping above the parapet is the brick gable end of the 1912 LYR cotton warehouse; being nearer to Knowsley Street, we obtain a close-up of the unimposing entrance to the station, complete with four advertising posters astride the two arched windows and the arched door. All this was caught on camera at 15.57, Saturday, 28th July 1962.
Eric Bentley(2)

This highly atmospheric view was taken at 22.00 on Friday, 10th February 1967, virtually at the end of steam-hauled trains in the Bury area. The photographer has taken a position at the western end of the Up platform at Knowsley Street Station and is facing the junction where the East Fork curves off to Bolton Street Station. Beyond Manchester Road bridge, the signalman has settled down on the late shift (22.00 to 06.00) as the 20.37 Oldham Clegg Street to Carnforth parcels awaits a clear road out of Bury. The "pair of eyes" are the rear side of two banner signals mounted on a right-hand bracket beneath Knowsley Street bridge. The footpath notice refers to the narrow path which ran alongside the East Fork enabling railway personnel to walk the short distance between the two stations.

Eric Bentley

At 18.35 on Tuesday, 10th May 1966, a west-bound freight train trundles through Knowsley Street Station hauled by an unidentified Stanier 8F. Following the two front vans is the 1960s version of containerisation. This kind of container had a corrugated end, one set of end doors, and one pair of doors on each side. It had a capacity of 5 tons, or 724 cubic feet. Behind the container wagon, is a 30 ton bogie bolster wagon loaded with rolled steel girders which are chained to the wagon to prevent movement. The Up side of the station exhibited two types of platform canopies: closest to the footbridge and attached to the brick building was a glazed ridge and furrow design. This was followed by a pitched roof canopy which originally extended as far as the northern end of the cotton warehouse. A rare glimpse of the yard behind the station reveals a siding curving across the sett-paved yard, and a Commer van parked with its rear end under the canopy where a stack of parcels awaits attention. Leading up to Knowsley Street is the covered incline, and partly glazed pedestrian walkway which connected the street entrance with the booking hall, situated at platform level. Note the concrete distance post leaning dejectedly against the inside of the paling fence, itself in need of repair, and the regularly-spaced set of gas lamps which are now considered to be collectors' items for front gardens.

Eric Bentley

Knowsley Street Station
- Footbridge Accident, 1952.

Knowsley Street Station was always considered to be Bury's second station. It was certainly unpopular with Bury folk, and today is only a memory in the minds of those who knew it, and probably for most, a now forgotten piece of the town's fabric which existed up to 1971. Apart from the many happy memories of people who started their annual holiday at the station, one occurrence alone has forged a place for it in the annals of local legend, a notoriety bordering on infamy. Bridge No.18 was the station's footbridge, a structure which nestled against the Liverpool and Bury Railway Company's 1848 stone bridge which carried Knowsley Street over the railway.

Saturday 19 January 1952 was just another soccer day in the calendar of Football Association fixtures. Bury were host to Blackburn Rovers at Gigg Lane. The match over, nearly 3000 away supporters headed for home via Knowsley Street Station where four trains had been laid on to convey them back to Blackburn and surrounding area. The trains allocated for the return journey were as follows: No.560, the 4.30pm to Gisburn; No.561, the 4.40pm; No.562, the 4.46pm; and 562A, the 4.55pm. The carriages for the first train arrived at the Down platform at 4.35, the actual departure time. A queue of supporters stretched from a gate at the foot of the stairs, over the bridge, into the booking hall, and along the covered approach as far as the main entrance on Knowsley Street. On arrival of train No.560, some 750 passengers were allowed to pass through the gate and enter the train, which

The **station footbridge at Knowsley Street** allowed for an interesting view of the station layout, looking east, on this occasion, on Wednesday, 27th December 1961. At 14.40, the photographer has caught on film a Stanier 8F, **48626** of Crewe shed, drawing a west-bound freight along the Down Slow line, the far end of the train of wagons having just passed Bury East signal box. Standing at the Up platform is the 14.30 Bacup to Manchester Victoria service in the hands of a Bury allocated Metro Cammel twin car set. This particular design was incompatible with other DMU sets and could not be coupled up in the event of breakdown or the need for extra capacity at rush hours. Because of this, this set and others like it, were worked on a regular route to obviate any problems. The assortment of roof styles at the station is once again clearly seen from the elevated vantage point. The variety was a product of station development by accretion over different periods, leading to a variety of shapes and sizes.   *Eric Bentley*

left at 4.38, eight minutes late. A number of passengers milled about on the Down platform, whilst the queue behind the down gate shuffled forwards in anticipation of the next train. Witnesses recalled that the queue was orderly in conduct; there was no stamping or jumping despite the high spirits of the away team: Blackburn had won the match two goals to nil.

As soon as the first train had departed, the gate was opened again to allow the queue to move forwards. It was the station master's intention *"to ensure that there would be no overcrowding and that the trains would be despatched in an orderly manner"*. It was at this juncture that Bridge No.18 collapsed through a height of 15 feet to rail level - *"...... the main beams from side to side came down just like a gigantic lift"*, said eyewitness. Two hundred people fell with the bridge which hit the rails in a cloud of dust, soot, and years of filth. One person was killed, and 173 injured, of whom 136 were conveyed to Bury General Hospital.

The station master, standing on the Down platform 80 yards away had heard the bridge timbers creaking, and, on turning and peering through the smoke, saw the bridge collapse. The signalman at Bury West box also saw the incident and immediately signalled "Obstruction Danger" to the signal boxes on either side. Immediate first aid was given by the station staff and other passengers. The police, fire brigade, and ambulances arrived at the scene in turn between 4.45 and 5pm.

The remaining supporters were directed to Bolton Street Station to which their trains had been diverted. The Newton Heath breakdown crane was sent for to help in clearing away the heaviest of the debris, but was cancelled when this had been cleared by 6.30pm for trains to pass through the station at caution. The crane was, however, sent for later to assist in the removal of the remaining portion of the bridge which was regarded as unsafe.

It was estimated that the footbridge had been erected some seventy years earlier. No records or drawings were found to ascertain the date. The covered bridge extended from a retaining wall which supported the booking hall on the Up side, to a brick abutment on the Down side. The total span was 72 feet 6 inches, but two cast iron columns on the Up platform reduced the clear span to 60 feet 9inches. It was this clear span which collapsed. The main structure consisted of two timber queen post trusses carrying a 4 inches thick timber flooring which rested on two timber booms. The trusses were supported on the above-mentioned cast iron columns on the Up side and built into the brick abutment on the Down side. The bridge was sheathed in boarding inside and outside the trusses, above which was a glazed roof. The load was taken by the queen posts and minor posts through a set of wrought iron straps which were originally 3¼ inches wide and 3/8 inches thick. Some of the original straps had been replaced sometime during the bridge's existence. It was the condition of these straps which had primarily contributed to the collapse of the bridge.

According to the Inspecting Officer: "*The straps holding the bottom booms to the vertical members were in a deplorable condition; every one of them was badly corroded and none had been carrying any load; in some cases all that was left were two short lengths of wasted metal hanging from the vertical member*".

The Inspecting Officer's report continued by stating that "*The bridge must have been in this dangerous condition for some years and it was only the precarious and fortuitous support given by the outside boarding which saved it from destruction for so long*". Despite examinations in 1944, 1945, 1948, and a repaint in 1949, cursory inspections had failed to notice the corroded condition of the straps and the evidence of timber decay. There had, however, been difficulties in examining the bridges thoroughly due to the boarding which had hidden any potential trouble. The apparent lack of maintenance over a period of ten to fifteen years was a point seized upon by the press which reported the accident in the days after. Headlines such as the following hit the nail on the head: "BRIDGE METAL CORRODED - NO PROPER INSPECTION FOR YEARS BEFORE COLLAPSE" [News Chronicle]; "JURY CRITICISES INSPECTION OF RAILWAY BRIDGE - METAL WORK VERY BADLY CORRODED" [Manchester Guardian].

The Knowsley Street footbridge had its counterpart at nearby Ramsbottom, and at Oldham. Following the accident at Bury, the bridge at Oldham was inspected and found to have corroded straps with some deterioration in the timber. The Oldham bridge was also boarded at the sides, and also underneath, a feature which had helped to protect the bridge from the sulphurous blasts. Even so it was found that the wrought iron straps had corroded to a depth of 1/8 inch. The bridge at Ramsbottom was boarded on the inside only so that inspection of the trusses and straps would have been rendered more easily.

A new footbridge was erected at Knowsley Street Station in 1953 in exactly the same position, this time employing steel, with a concrete deck, and generous glazing to allow ingress of natural light. This bridge was dismantled and removed in 1971 during the demolition of the station.

This photograph perhaps, more than any other, illustrates the character and atmosphere of **Knowsley Street Station**. The occasion is marked by the Manchester Rail Travel and Severn Valley Railway Society's joint tour of the north of England. The tour began at Birmingham and included the following towns in the North of England: Stockport, Buxton, Huddersfield, Sowerby Bridge, Blackburn, Bolton, Rochdale, and Liverpool. Special 1Z77 has arrived at Bury on Saturday, 20th April 1968, at 15.48, next stop Rochdale, and drawn by an immaculate Stanier 8F **48773** (Bolton shed). This scene, in particular, shows the pronounced "Bury Hollow" to the west of the station; the kink in the eleven-coach train coincides with the arch of Manchester Road bridge. As a touch of modernity, colour light signals had been installed at the station over the Down lines, the actual date of installation remaining uncertain. *Eric Bentley*

The photographer has taken his position on the Down Fast line to obtain a view of the aftermath of the collapse of Bridge No.18. A group of workmen is engaged in discussion on the barrow crossing approximately below the point where the bridge had fallen. A jagged section of the bottom boom projects outwards from the cast iron columns on the Up platform, a grim reminder of the tragedy which had occurred not many hours earlier. Debris has been cleared from the running lines, some of it now stacked at each end of the platforms, awaiting removal. Some of this formed specimens for testing for the research department of The Railway Executive in March 1952. A good view of the masonry bridge with its year of erection could be made from the station after the accident; today, it can be viewed from the car park adjacent to Knowsley Street. ***Authors collection***

The January sunshine picks out the details of the iron work which supported the canopy over the Down platform, and that over the western end of the ridge and furrow roof on the Up side. It is a common enough experience of strangeness when a familiar, very much taken-for-granted feature suddenly disappears from view - the gap it leaves then becomes for a time a focus of interest. So it appears for the group of men standing on the Up platform as a Stanier 2-6-4 tank engine, number **42429**, makes its way slowly along the Up Slow line into the station. The two signs facing the platforms informing that PASSENGERS MUST NOT CROSS THE LINE EXCEPT BY THE BRIDGE now seem irrelevant. ***Authors collection***

The wrought iron gates at the foot of the footbridge staircase, which led the passengers to and from the Down platform, are now firmly locked on the 25 January 1952, six days after the accident. These were the gates which Mr G U Gray, the Station Master, had sought to control the movement of the queue on to the platform and into the waiting train immediately before the accident. Note the Train Departure poster which has been affixed to an inveterate LMS notice board, this in itself a relict feature of a bygone period of railway history.

A view of the second flight of stairs which led up to the footbridge proper from the Down platform. The brick wall at the head of the stairs formed part of the abutment which had supported the footbridge on the Down side. This portion of the bridge came in for special comment by the Inspecting Officer in his report when he referred to the ends of the Down side trusses which were partially enclosed by the brick abutment, "so that damp seeped into the timber encased in the bearings and set up serious decay". Close observation shows the effect of the passage of millions of boots and shoes on the treads of the staircase.

No photographs are known to exist of the interior of the old footbridge, but from June 1953 onwards, this view would meet those passengers heading for the Down platform from the booking hall. The steel construction in place of timber gives it a clean and reassuring look. The glazing faced only on to the station leaving the blank side closest to the stonework of Knowsley Street bridge decorated with railway posters. Despite the new order of things, British Railways held on to its tried and trusted gas mantles for illumination, three of which can be seen close to the bracing beneath the roof.

British Railways (LMR)

A general view of the replacement footbridge which was erected in the early months of 1953. The photographer was standing at the western end of the Up platform and has captured not only the new footbridge but also the Manchester Road stone arch, the Intersection Bridge carrying the Clifton Junction to Accrington line in the distance, and a glimpse of the front of Bury West signal box. Peeping over the parapet of Knowsley Street bridge is the top of Jubilee Clock Tower, a familiar landmark in the area, and one which has seen many changes through the passage of time. The date of the photograph is 27 January 1954. *British Railways (LMR)*

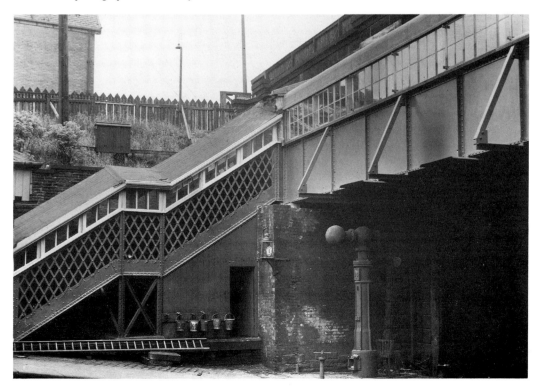

This photograph was taken on the 19 June 1953 showing the **Down side portion of the new Bridge No.18**, and the original covered staircase leading up to it. A few features of the new bridge were different to the old one, namely, the new style of glazing (it was possible to open several of the windows), the angled steel outriggers (or strengtheners), and the steel smoke deflectors designed to protect the base of the bridge from the sulphurous attack of smoke blasts from locomotive chimneys. Below the bridge water column No.15 stands at the foot of the platform ramp: when the accident occurred, the end of the old bridge fell on to this column, momentarily arresting its fall to the tracks. Near to the bridge number plate there is a bracket holding a pendant gas light, its meagre candle-power supposedly sufficient to illuminate the doorway of the store room beneath the staircase, and the row of fire buckets alongside.

An evening scene at Knowsley Street Station, 10th May 1966. Black 5 **45341** (Newton Heath shed) stands in the Up Bay with train number 3J07, the 17.55 Bacup to Rochdale parcels train. This train spent just over half an hour at the station (between 18.37 and 19.12) while parcels were loaded and unloaded. Today, such loads are sent by road, adding to the congestion on the M62 and in the town centres. On the Down Fast line is an unidentified Black 5 slowly approaching the colour light signal which indicates red. The ex-LYR 1912 cotton warehouse presents a solid and enduring face towards the station; in fact it had only five more years of existence before it was razed to the ground. Note the rows of gas lamps along each platform - gas lamps and colour light signals make for an interesting contrast in technology at the station, which appears to be devoid of passengers. The Up Bay platform at which the parcels train is standing was to be closed, along with several sidings, in June 1969.   *Eric Bentley*

Knowsley Street passenger and goods station as seen from Market Street bridge, fifty minutes after noon, Wednesday, 20th February 1963. The only sign of activity is the passage of a coal train hauled by an unidentified Austerity 2-8-0 en route to Agecroft Power Station with Yorkshire coal via Bury Loop. The full width of the cotton warehouse can now be appreciated in this view: it was not the only warehouse serving the goods station, but it was the largest. In fact, the "L&Y Yard", as it was also known, was of no mean size, being able to accommodate over 400 wagons. Amongst the many railway features to be seen mention must be made of the structures for the provision of water supply to locomotives: at least three water columns are evident in addition to the parachute type water column, right of centre. Note, too, the fogman's concrete refuge, and the yard lamps mounted on tall posts. From its place in Tower Gardens, the ornate Whitehead Memorial Clock Tower overlooks all; erected just before the Great War, it watched over the station as it reached its zenith, suffered decline, and was ultimately erased from Bury's landscape.

Eric Bentley

East of the station in full use at 12.45, Wednesday, 4th May 1962. Austerity **90729** (Bolton shed) waits at the Up Goods line signal with a long rake of east-bound coal empties, possibly on the Aintree Sidings to Crofton Hall run. Leaving the passenger station, is named Black 5, **45156** *Ayrshire Yeomanry* of Newton Heath shed with the 12.30Sx Bolton to Rochdale local service. Arriving at the Down platform is the 12.30Sx Rochdale to Bolton train, care of a DMU, displaying its high visibility whiskers and tail lights. In this view, we can see the smaller goods shed which was situated behind its larger neighbour, and the lightweight gantries which spanned the yard from which several electric lights were suspended. Bury East signal box, like many others, has bricked-up locking room windows, a legacy from the war years. the lever frame and block system instruments faced on to the yard. The cabin was opened by the LYR in 1898 as No.374. Peeping between two yard lamps is the front end of a Scammell Scarab, minus trailer.

Eric Bentley

An evening summer sun glances down on a busy scene close to Bury East signal box, on the 9th August 1963. Awaiting a clear road at the Down Fast signal is an unidentified Black 5 which was recorded by the photographer as possibly having come off the Bacup to Rochdale parcels train; approaching the station on the Up Fast line is a Castleton to Bury train of vans drawn by a Crab; proceeding tender first on the Up line of the Bury Loop is Fowler **44096**, taking the 18.22 Radcliffe North to Bury Knowsley Street Goods traffic; far left, another Fowler, **43880** travels light engine to Bury shed, this engine being one of five stabled at Bury. In the distance, Manchester Road tunnel marks the lowest point of the Bury Loop, beyond which the gradient climbs towards Bury Loco Junction. It now of course forms part of the alignment taking Metrolink from Bury Interchange. A small corner of the slated roof of Bury East signal box intrudes on to the scene whilst notice must be made of the steel gantry bearing four dolls spanning the Down lines. The ladder end of the gantry has been provided with a tall electric lamp to cast a welcome light to assist footplate crews access to the signal box in the dark when their train was detained at the gantry stop signals. The north-easterly aspect of Bury High School - now Peel Sixth Form College - lies in shadow as the evening sunlight pales. The photograph was taken on most people's end of the working week, Friday, at 18.40.

Eric Bentley

Leaving Knowsley Street. Marking its presence as it leaves the station, BR Standard 4MT **75018** (Southport shed) continues the journey with the 12.30 all-stations to Rochdale from Bolton. An assortment of wagons stand in the goods yard, including a small container which is loaded on a Scammell trailer. Telegraph poles have long since vanished from the railway scene; this one is unusual in having not only eleven arms bearing lines in one direction, but also fourteen arms at right-angles, bearing telephone lines and signalling circuits to Bury East Signal Box across the tracks - a veritable junction pole! Note the modern control boxes at the base of the signal gantry, the line of concrete troughing which requires completion, and the point-rodding and signal wires running parallel to the Down Slow line towards the station. Time and date: 12.45, Wednesday, 20th February 1963.

Eric Bentley

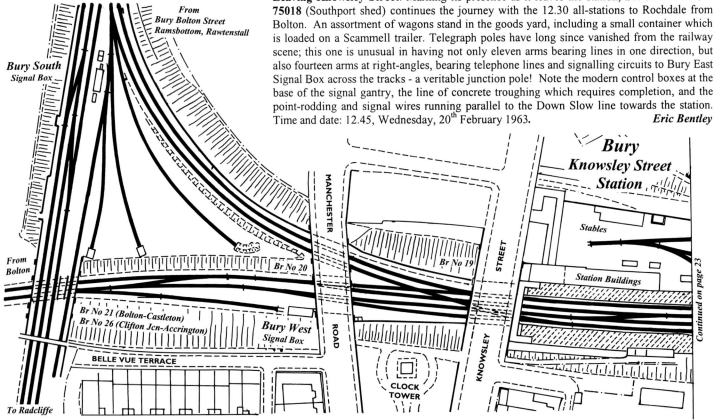

From
Bury Bolton Street
Ramsbottom, Rawtenstall

Bury South
Signal Box

From
Bolton

Br No 21 (Bolton-Castleton)
Br No 26 (Clifton Jcn-Accrington)

Br No 20

Br No 19

Bury West
Signal Box

BELLE VUE TERRACE

To Radcliffe

MANCHESTER ROAD

CLOCK
TOWER

KNOWSLEY STREET

Bury
Knowsley Street
Station

Stables

Station Buildings

Continued on page 23

Early afternoon, and a bright one too, on Monday, 5th April 1965. Facing west towards Market Street bridge we have two examples of activity in the form of a Black 5, **45437** (Agecroft) drawing forward with a pick-up freight out of Knowsley Street Goods Yard. Meanwhile, the driver of Ivatt **46412** is engaged in the routine oiling of his engine which is impatiently blowing off while engaged on the more menial task of shunting. Somewhere in the expanse of buildings beyond the railway was the Co-op Bakery noted for its appetising aroma of freshly baked bread.   *Eric Bentley*

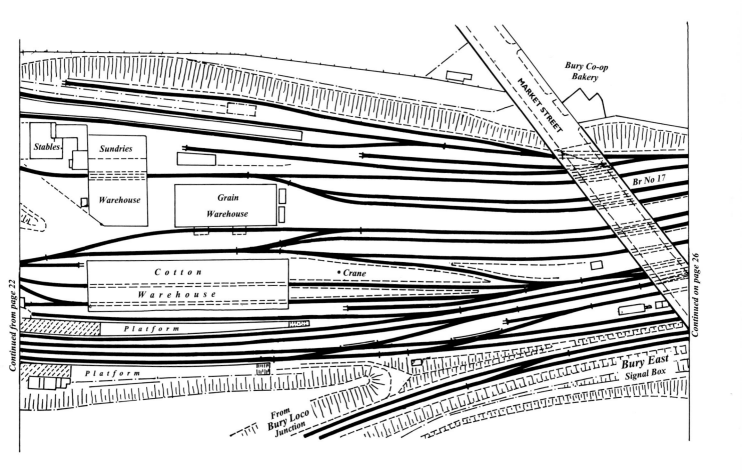

Early morning start! The photographer has found a spot on the northern side of the railway, in an area locally known as Townside Fields, a few hundred yards from Market Street bridge. On this occasion, the 07.26 Bank Holiday special (reporting number 1X24) is carrying holiday makers from the Rossendale area and Ramsbottom. Its route from the latter place has brought the train through Bolton Street Station, down the East Fork, and through Knowsley Street Station, en route for London Marylebone. The greater part of the journey to the Metropolis, has of course, still to be done, on 6th July 1963.

Eric Bentley

From the same spot at Townside Fields, we see Crab **42680** (Agecroft shed) as she opens her safety valve at 07.10 on Saturday, 6th July 1963, in making her way along the Up line towards Broadfield. The profile of Market Street bridge is impressive: at this point the public highway had to be carried over the main lines, several goods lines, and the Loop lines. The goods train is passing under the girder span of 59 feet over the Up Main lines, erected in 1880; there are also four arched spans carrying the road over the sidings, also erected in 1880; and finally, two cast iron girder bridges over the Loop lines, each of 26 feet 4 ins span, erected in 1898 to accommodate the Bury Connecting Line (Loop Line). In November 1967 it was announced that *"The goods yard and marshalling sidings will be taken out of use....."* and that *"The arms of all associated signals will be taken away."* With this threat of closure, a major feature of Bury's railway infrastructure was to be swept away.

Eric Bentley

It was unusual to find an Austerity locomotive - often dubbed as "WD's"- in a well turned-out condition. There is however, always an exception; 90110 makes a pleasing sight, and is a credit to the cleaners at its home shed, Bolton - assuming, of course, that they were responsible. The engine stands on the Up Through line adjacent to a stone retaining wall near the saw mills which lay off Heywood Street North. Note the "Lion and Wheel" emblem on the tender, an image adopted by British Railways in the 1950s. Beyond are the houses which lined Frank Street, with those of Edward Street stretching at right-angles towards the centre of the town, still, in the 1960s, gas-lit and grateful for it. Through the cab side window we have a glimpse of the fireman, his grease - top cap, the traditional headgear for thousands of footplate men. **90110** was built by the North British Company in 1943, having the distinction of being included in Netherlands Railway stock before its return to Britain. *Eric Bentley*

Bury shed's Crab 42700 approaches Knowsley Street Station from Rochdale with a football special for the FA Cup-Tie between Division 3 Bury, and Division 1 Bolton, a match which took place on Saturday, 9th March 1960. The all-ticket game was played, of course, at the Gigg Lane ground, the match resulting in a one-all draw, watched by a high-capacity crowd of 35,000. The return match was played on Wednesday, 13th March at Burnden Park, Bolton, the latter club winning on its home ground 4 - 2 after extra time. Exciting times! Returning to a railway theme, far left we see Ivatt **46414,** apparently cleaned up for the occasion, and occupying itself shunting in the sidings. Bottom left shows a fogman's timber hut; note the look-out hole in the side, and the wheel arrangement alongside the hut which operated the detonator placer. A spread of terraced houses line East Street and Frank Street in an area of Bury which had its fair share of industry in the form of cotton mills and small businesses. The roof of Holy Trinity Church rises above the rows of chimney stacks, whilst in the foreground, the Bury Loop begins its descent to Manchester Road Tunnel.

Eric Bentley

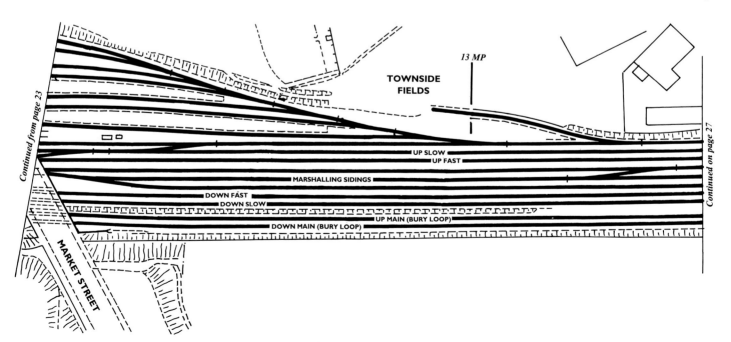

Continued from page 23

TOWNSIDE
FIELDS

13 MP

UP SLOW
UP FAST
MARSHALLING SIDINGS
DOWN FAST
DOWN SLOW
UP MAIN (BURY LOOP)
DOWN MAIN (BURY LOOP)

MARKET STREET

Continued on page 27

From Market Street bridge the view east looked like this, with Heywood Street bridge and the original single arch in the near distance. Bridge No.16 had three spans: the stone arch had a span of 24feet 9ins over the Up lines; the cast iron girder bridge of span 26feet over the Down lines; and the 1898 extension for the Loop lines also of cast iron, spanning 26feet. The Loop line continued double track parallel to the main line between Market Street and Heywood Street bridges, not joining the main line until passing under the latter bridge as will be 'seen later. At 18.40, Friday, 9th August 1963, we have an Ivatt 2MT shunting, and mostly hidden by the rake vans; a Crab leaving the yard on a Bacup to Moston Sidings goods train; a Black 5 proceeding apace along the Up Main line with a Nelson to Moston Sidings vans. A single Austerity light engine occupies a siding.in front of the arch of Heywood Street bridge. Recent ballasting work has taken place judging by the quantity of clean ballast seen in the photograph.

Eric Bentley

WILSON STREET

HEYWOOD STREET

UP SLOW
UP FAST

Br No 16

DOWN FAST
DOWN SLOW

UP MAIN (BURY LOOP)

DOWN MAIN (BURY LOOP)

Bury Loop Junction
Signal Box

Continued on page 28

A busy scene captured on camera, the photographer looking over the parapet of Heywood Street bridge on the 6th October 1965. Black 5 44928 carries out its shunting duties to the east of Knowsley Street L&Y Goods Depot, and provides a few minutes rest for the permanent way workers. Today, The Health and Safety Executive would not countenance the absence of high-visibility apparel which, in the mid-1960s, was regarded as completely normal. Left on an intermediate siding between the Up and Down Main lines is a train of 16 ton mineral wagons each containing a full load of coal, the rake complete with the inevitable guard's van at the rear. The bridge in the distance carries Market Street, remarkable for the number of spans required to carry the thoroughfare across the main running lines and an expanse of sidings.   *Ray Farrell*

(Right) One of Bolton shed's work-horses in the form of Austerity 90110, in a more usual work-stained condition, heads off towards Heap Bridge with an assortment of coal wagons. In 1958, when this photograph was taken, it was customary either to run such trains loose-coupled, reliance being placed entirely on the efficiency of the locomotive brake power, along with those of the brake van in the rear, or for the train to be partially vacuum braked. In order to ensure that break-away wagons and other rolling stock did not run back down an incline, thereby fouling the main line at a set of points, catch-points were positioned to derail them. Such was the case at Bury Loop Junction where the Down line of the Loop left the main line.
Eric Bentley

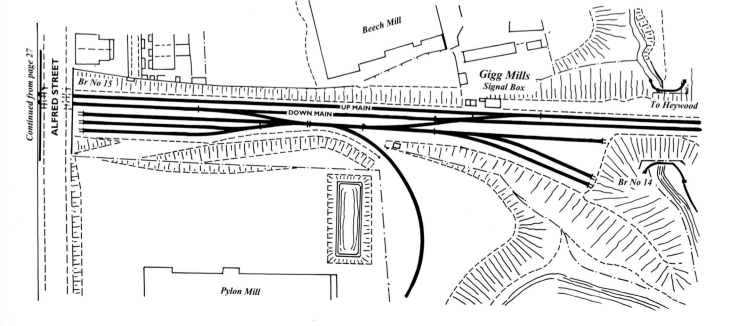

Continued from page 27

ALFRED STREET

Br No 15

Beech Mill

Gigg Mills
Signal Box

DOWN MAIN   UP MAIN

To Heywood

Br No 14

Pylon Mill

Early evening, in early September 1964. An unidentified Black 5 pulls away from Bury past Bury Loop Junction with a Wigan Wallgate to Rochdale all-stations passenger train. In the distance is bridge No.15, with its arched span of 24 feet 9 ins thrown across the railway to carry Alfred Street. Note how the Up line of the Bury Loop joins the Up Main line towards Heywood and Rochdale via the diamond crossing over the Down Main. Although the photograph portrays a semi-rural ambience, the tall chimney marks the position of the Beech Cotton Mill, while off to the right, and out of sight in this view, was the CWS Pylon Mill. The closeness of industrial land use in areas such as Gigg and Pimhole to the east of central Bury are never far away, the railway cutting a swathe through both places. A young Jeff Wells remembers sitting hour after hour on the side of a grassy cutting similar to this in the 1950s, watching a seemingly endless procession of trains pass by between Middleton Junction and Moston.

The view eastwards at Bury Loop Junction in early September 1964. A Radcliffe to Knowsley Street Goods trip freight, hauled by **0-6-0 4F No 43913,** a Fowler Midland design, awaits the passage of the 17.15 Nelson to Moston Sidings van train to clear the junction. When this has been accomplished, the trip freight will obey the calling-on, or subsidiary, signal (mounted on the lower part of the lattice post of the stop signal) and proceed forward on to the Up Main line until the last wagon has cleared the points; then the trip freight will reverse "bang road" until the goods yard is reached. This manoeuvre was a regular one. The catch-point post (which can be seen *in the above picture* with a distinctive lean in front the bridge) should at least indicate to the observer that the line at this location was on a rising gradient out of Bury. **Eric Bentley**

On a sunny spring day, Austerity **90854** has stopped at Bury Loop Junction stop signal and is about to set back into Knowsley Street Goods Yard. Those with good eyesight, or with the aid of a magnifying glass, will no doubt notice the ground-signal positioned several yards beyond the signal box, giving a clear road westwards. The rake of mixed wagons is a short one suggesting that 90854 was engaged in shunting when caught on camera, Thursday, 26th March 1964. *Ray Farrell*

By the mid-1960s it was rare to see a well-turned out steam locomotive. Near the end of steam, few cared about the appearance of the machines which were destined for scrap. Here is a perfect example of the lack of care and maintenance; a Black 5 which has not felt the touch of an oily rag for some time. No. **45202** has a slight leak from its cylinder as she draws past Bury Loop Junction on the 22nd April 1965. As far as can be seen, the train is a short one comprising a van, a sheet wagon, a bogie-bolster, and a container in an open wagon. Note the calling-on signal for attaching banking engines, below the stop signal, the latter indicating a clear road ahead for the journey onwards to Heywood. *Ray Farrell*

Bury Loop Junction signal box was positioned between the Up and Down lines on the eastern side of bridge No.16, Heywood Street bridge. It was opened in 1898 as LYR No.373 in connection with the Connecting Line from Loco Junction, at Buckley Wells. Unfortunately, this box met an untimely and ignoble end by catching fire on the 24th March 1967. In this view we see the box fully functioning as Jubilee class **45592** *Indore* (Carnforth shed) storms past with the 08.50 Liverpool Exchange to Scarborough service, on Saturday, 15th August 1964. Worthy of mention are the ash and coal bins at the foot of the signal box steps, the platelayers' hut close to the bridge, the LMS right-hand offset bracket signal, and the tall lattice post which controlled the exit from the Up Loop line. The diagonal stripe on the cab side indicated to footplate men and others that the locomotive was not to be used on the electrified lines south of Crewe due to the lack of clearance between the cab roof and overhead catenary.

Eric Bentley

The signalman takes a breath of smoke-filled air at the door of his cabin as Black 5 **44674** (Carlisle Kingmoor) makes a quick and smoky departure form Knowsley Street Station at 13.13, Saturday, 16th July 1966, with 1N97, the Blackpool North to Halifax relief train. Bury Loop Junction box possessed an LYR 48 lever frame, comprising 37 working levers and 11 spare, before its demise by fire. The modification to the cabin's chimney by adding an extension to the brick stack was probably made to enhance the flue draught and to eliminate a smoky interior. On the 9th April 1967 it was officially announced that the remains of the signal box would be demolished and that the arms of all signals worked from it would be taken away. Closure actually took place on the 15th April. The junction points near the box leading to and from Loop Junction were secured in the normal position pending the closure of the Loop line. *Eric Bentley*

A weak autumn sunlight highlights the tender of Black 5 **45318** as she travels tender first from the Bury Loop line and on to the Up Main line towards Heap Bridge Junction. Three chemical tank wagons - a light load for a class 5MT engine - are also highlighted by the sun: the short-wheelbase 20 ton vehicles are painted silver, or light grey, with a red solebar, this being in accordance with Board of Trade regulations concerning traffic of inflammable liquids. Although no firm details are known about the destination of this train, it is speculation as to whether it is destined for Heap Bridge Goods Depot, or to set back into Knowsley Street Goods, "bang road" when clear of the points on the Up Main line. The date is the 22nd November 1965.

Framed by the black interior of Alfred Street bridge, a Rochdale-bound Cravens 2-car DMU takes the Up line away from Bury Loop Junction on the 22nd April 1965. The facing ground or disc signal applied to trains setting back from the Down Main line into the Loop line, seen bearing off to the left. The rear side of a similar disc signal which applied to the cross-over from the Down Main to the Up Main line can be seen behind the other.

Both: *Ray Farrell*

"Crab" 42711 (Wigan shed) storms out of Bury under Alfred Street bridge with the 12.30 Bolton Trinity Street Station to Rochdale service, on Wednesday, 1st May 1963. At this location, the track work is quite simple after the complexity of the junctions, goods lines, and sidings just outside Knowsley Street Station. Two plain lines are visible: the train is travelling on the Up Main line for Heywood and Rochdale, the "up" direction taken towards Manchester; the other line is the Down Main from Manchester in the Bolton direction. It may be relevant here to mention that the Horwich Crab was a curious mixture of two designs: a Horwich engine, designed by George Hughes, and a Fowler Midland tender which was a misfit, since it was 18 inches narrower that the engine. This characteristic feature of Crabs can be discerned by comparing the cab side with the front of the tender. For the whole of their working days the Crabs were to pull this narrower, and, incidentally, heavier tender (when full of coal) on their multifarious journeys.

Eric Bentley

A locomotive with a purpose - Fowler Midland type 43913 unashamedly spreads a generous coating of soot over the Monday morning washing and windows as she hurries towards Heap Bridge Junction. This wanton act of railway inconsideration occurred at 12.10, 5th March 1962, at the site of Gigg Mill Sidings. Those with a keen eye will spot the line side gradient post, the nearer arm of which is correctly inclined upwards thereby indicating the 1 in 85 uphill gradient. A disc of a ground signal with its face towards Heap Bridge can also be spotted slightly above rail level. This signal controlled movements over a connection from the Up Main line to the Down Main line, situated a few yards east of Alfred Street bridge, the latter totally obscured by the large volume of drifting smoke. *Eric Bentley*

An unidentified Crab stops and awaits assistance beyond Alfred Street bridge. The gradient at this point is now climbing at 1 in 85 through a distance of 2 ½ miles, so that heavy freight trains needed the assistance of a banking engine. At 18.15, Friday, 10th August 1962, we see such an occasion when the 15.10 Accrington to Moston Sidings Class E freight required a banker. The first seven wagons are conflats which are conveying small containers. Just beyond the engine are the remains of Gigg Mills signal box. The box opened in 1899 as LYR 372 with a 30 lever frame; it was constructed to control movements to and from Gigg Mill Siding which opened on the 14th June 1899. Closure of Gigg Mills box has been estimated to have taken place between 1936 and 1940, the lack of precise dates contributing to the enigma of this particular box. The LMS broad flanged beam balanced bracket signal is of interest. All the stop signals were controlled by Bury Loop Junction box, and all the distants controlled by Bury East box. The two boards (signals) on the right were for trains to travel down the Bury Loop line; those on the taller middle doll were for the Slow or platform line at Knowsley Street Station; whilst those on the left applied to the Down Fast line through the station. The small board on this latter doll was a subsidiary signal applying to the same line. The signals on the middle doll are off for an approaching 18.05 Dmu service between Rochdale and Bolton, the train just visible as it passes Heap Bridge Junction.

Eric Bentley

Looking west towards Alfred Street bridge, at 10.04, Saturday, 28th July 1962, the photographer has caught BR Standard 4-6-0 5MT **73139** (Rowsley shed) as she takes the gradient in her stride with the 08.50 Liverpool Exchange to Scarborough, Saturdays only service, next stop Rochdale. 73139 was one of a batch of 172 locomotives designed at Doncaster in 1951 by BR as one of twelve standard designs which were planned for future construction before the decision of 1956 to abandon steam propulsion. This particular engine was one of thirty of the class fitted with Caprotti valve gear. The reporting number 1J01 has been chalked below the smoke-box door, probably an expedient adopted when no official indicator panel was available. Note the pronounced "dip" of the line beneath the bridge.

Eric Bentley

With the aid of a banker in the form of 0-6-0 4F, **44096**, a Bury shed engine, the Accrington to Moston Sidings goods is moving forward. This location, on the Down side where the photographer is standing, marks the approximate position of where the long-removed Gigg Mills Siding curved off to the right. The siding stretched south as a single line with passing loops for a distance of about 600 yards, serving the Co-op's Pilot Mill, and the Bury Paper Making Company, whose private siding agreement with the LYR dated back to the 22nd of November 1898. Beneath the recumbent telegraph pole there are both impressions of sleepers in the ground although the tell-tale signs of the siding itself are not visible due to the subsequent disturbance of the ground conditions over the years. The wall of the Beech Cotton Mill can be seen extending to the left of the rear end of the train.

Eric Bentley

An unidentified Austerity heads for Broadfield and Heywood with a lengthy train of empty 16 ton mineral wagons - an afternoon treat for the train watcher at 13.00, Thursday, 20th February 1964. Officially, this was train number 7N52, the 09.45 Aintree Sidings returning to Crofton Hall, and seen here making the climb out of Bury look easy. In this photograph taken above Barn Brook and School Street, we have a clear view of a nearby sign which had something to say but is unfortunately not near enough to read its message.

Eric Bentley

A long-distance and fascinating view of a forty-van train heading towards Heap Bridge Junction at 13.30, Saturday, 16th July 1966. The river Roch at this point forms a natural boundary between Heywood and Bury, the line of division running along the middle of the river as the latter meanders through both open and farmed land. Beyond the railway is a Lowry-type landscape representing Bury's eastern districts of Pimhole and Gigg, districts dominated by mill and factory chimneys, intermixed with ranks of terraced housing. The church spire (left) is that of St. Mary's, Market Place, in the town centre, while over on the right is the square water tank tower of Pimhole Mills. Taking centre stage is the dark Beech Mill chimney, presiding over the whole area. Not only was the sight of such a train passing a common enough occurrence in the 1960s, but so too was the sound of many wheels running over steel jointed rails - a distinctive and evocative sound which lingered on long after the train had passed by, especially at night.
Eric Bentley

Leaving Bury

Springs Branch engine 45073 hauls an eight-coach train out of Bury past the site of Gigg Mills signal box on its journey between Liverpool Exchange and Scarborough, the time of morning being 10.05, Saturday, 22nd June 1963. At the foot of the photograph is bridge No.14, a distinctive L&Y structure through the base of the embankment, the 19feet 6ins span which bore School Street and Barn Brook; the latter being a tributary of the river Roch. A prominent post with a disc at the top, and leaning a little to one side, marks the position of the bridge on the embankment.
Eric Bentley

Leading the same freight train, Stanier 8F has now reached Seven Arches viaduct over the river Roch. The viaduct was constructed in 1862 to replace an earlier timber structure, the contract being let to Thomas Broadbent of Strangeways, Manchester, for £3,491, reduced from a higher tender "by the altered method of fixing the centres". In order to keep the traffic moving while work was in progress, single line working was adopted. The new brick viaduct was opened on the 11th November 1862 "after a severe test by two of the most powerful engines the Company possesses, when all appeared quite safe". Note the uneven surface of the ground which forms the embankment, evidence of the way the spoil was tipped out of the contractors wagons during the construction of the railway; material for the same was taken from the nearby Spout Bank Cutting further up the line towards Heywood. The nature of the material (a sandy loam) was such that instead of building up it tended to spread out in lobes of wet uneven humps. Forming an interesting urban background, we can see, from left to right, California Iron Works, the windows of a cotton mill catching the light from the south, the spire of St. Thomas' Church, and the tower of St. Paul's Church. In the foreground are part of the filter beds of Heap Bridge Sewage Treatment Works which belonged to Heywood Corporation.

Almost at the end of the 2 ½ mile climb out of Bury, an unidentified Black 5 reaches Heap Bridge Junction with an east-bound freight comprising 40 wagons, and thought to have been on a Carlisle to Oldham (Glodwick Road) run. Heap Bridge Junction signal box opened as LYR No.371 in 1900 with a 20 lever frame (14 working and 6 spare), replacing an 1875 vintage box which had been located on the Down side. The box in view here was damaged by fire on the 3rd January 1971 and closed in March the same year. The occupation bridge (No.12) bore Water Fold (as it still does), a lane between Heap Bridge and neighbouring Pilsworth. Although appearing quite narrow, the arched bridge had a 19 feet 3 ins span. Close inspection of the bridge on foot reveals evidence that it was extended lengthways, the work carried out in 1876 when the Heap Bridge Branch was constructed along with a handful of sidings off the Up line behind the signal box.
Both Photos: Eric Bentley

Seven Arches

Seven Arches viaduct presents a sombre picture from the less photographed northern side. Here the 08.05 Sx Southport to Rochdale semi-fast service ascends the 1 in 85 incline towards Heywood. This was caught on camera at 09.15 on Thursday, 3rd March 1966. At the head of the three coach train is a BR Standard locomotive. *Eric Bentley*

Whenever photographing, or simply looking at **Seven Arches Viaduct**, the river Roch is never far away. In spelling the word in this way, deference is made to those who hail from Rochdale; on the other hand, if deference is made to those who reside in Bury, then the name should appear as Roach. Whichever spelling is used, the pleasant spot shown in this view conjures up the song, "Gone Fishing", the tranquillity of a summer's afternoon disturbed briefly by the passage of a Cravens Dmu. During 1999, the viaduct underwent major repairs which cost in the region of £300,000, the contractor being the Oldham-based firm of George Dew. The date of the photograph, taken on that languid day, is the 9th July 1966. *Ray Farrell*

A mist hangs over the river in the early morning (07.26) of the 26th August 1964. Passing into Heap Bridge Junction is a three-coach train on the 05.50 Liverpool Exchange to Rochdale all-stations service. Those readers with time to spare have an opportunity to count the number of mole hills in the foreground, or, as an alternative, consider who would have need to leave Liverpool at 05.50 to travel anywhere. Answers to both questions to the author via the publisher please.
Eric Bentley

At 10 o'clock on Saturday, 11th May 1963, Stanier 2-6-4 **42565** (Bolton shed) brings the 08.20 Blackpool Central to Rochdale service past Heap Bridge Junction. The remaining coaches of the train were taken off at Bolton and continued to Manchester Victoria as a different train. This photograph provides an excellent study of Heap Bridge signal box in its final years. All visible locking-room windows (below the operating floor) are intact, as are the two finials at either end of the roof-ridge. At the foot of the box (facing the camera) is a small aperture from which the signal wires left the box to run over scores of wooden or metal pulley stakes to their associated signal along the line. A semblance of modernisation appears in the form of steel location cases housing lineside electrical signalling equipment, and the concrete fogman's hut close to the apex of the timber fencing. The curious structure at the rear of the signal box with four legs and a pitched corrugated roof is also a modern addition to the scene. Its purpose is left to the imagination of the reader.
Eric Bentley

At 13.00, on Friday, 10th April 1964, this riverine setting records the passage of a long train of mineral wagons drawn by an Austerity 2-8-0 over Seven Arches and onwards to Heap Bridge Junction. A careful tally of the wagons reveals that there were no less than twenty eight 16 ton steel wagons in tow, not counting the guard's van at the tail end. A guard's van at the end of a goods train, long or short, fully fitted with a vacuum brake system or not, was the usual arrangement. Even with the emergence of diesel locomotives, a trade union agreement for the guard to travel in the rear cab had not been achieved, and so the time-honoured practice of the guard sitting in his van continued until the end of steam.

Eric Bentley

The climb of 1 in 85 from Alfred Street bridge does not ease until Broadfield Air Ministry Sidings are reached. An Austerity at the head of this 54 wagon train is blowing off as it reaches Heap Bridge signal box, the guard's van just clearing the eastern end of Seven Arches Viaduct. The small cluster of buildings perched on a hillock in front of the train comprise Spout Bank Farm. Today, the M66 motorway severs the embankment where the tall Up signal (which is off for the goods train) was positioned. Agreement for the proposed severance of the embankment dates back to the 21st September 1972 when the land was sold to the Department of the Environment. Bridge No.12A now carries the ELR line over the M66. Date and time of photograph: Thursday, 20th February 1964, at 13.00.

Eric Bentley

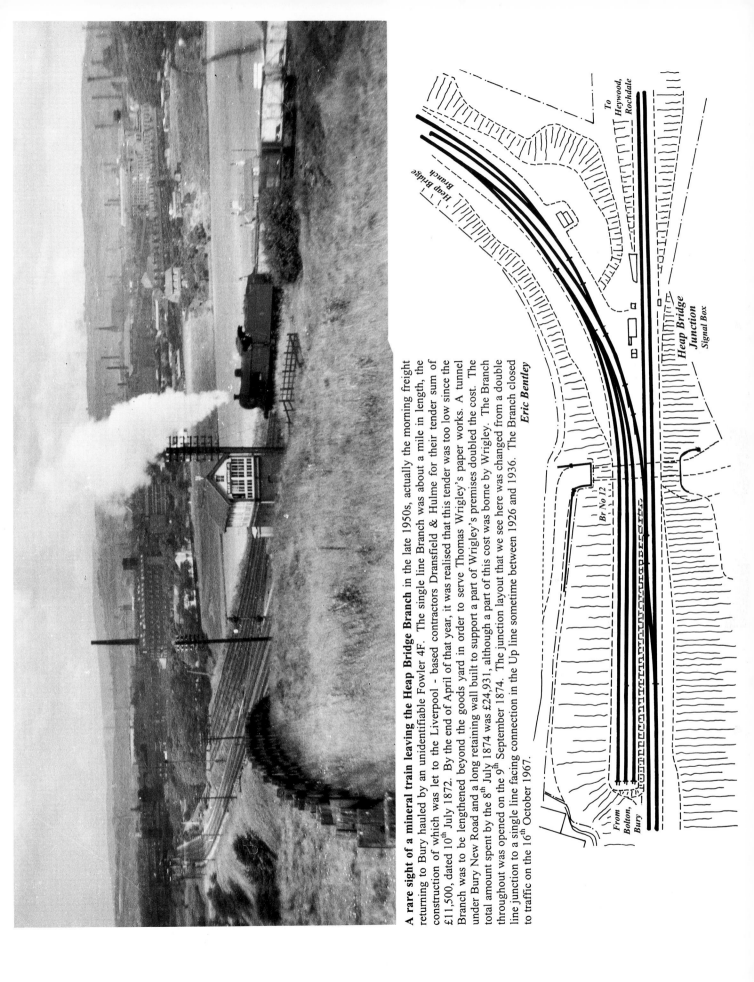

A rare sight of a mineral train leaving the Heap Bridge Branch in the late 1950s, actually the morning freight returning to Bury hauled by an unidentifiable Fowler 4F. The single line Branch was about a mile in length, the construction of which was let to the Liverpool - based contractors Dransfield & Hulme for their tender sum of £11,500, dated 10th July 1872. By the end of April of that year, it was realised that this tender was too low since the Branch was to be lengthened beyond the goods yard in order to serve Thomas Wrigley's paper works. A tunnel under Bury New Road and a long retaining wall built to support a part of Wrigley's premises doubled the cost. The total amount spent by the 8th July 1874 was £24,931, although a part of this cost was borne by Wrigley. The Branch throughout was opened on the 9th September 1874. The junction layout that we see here was changed from a double line junction to a single line facing connection in the Up line sometime between 1926 and 1936. The Branch closed to traffic on the 16th October 1967.

Eric Bentley

To
Heywood,
Rochdale

Heap Bridge
Branch

Heap Bridge
Junction
Signal Box

Br No 12

From
Bolton,
Bury

(Above) Stanier "Black Five" 44836 (Stockport shed) speeds past Heap Bridge Junction box to enter Spout Bank Cutting. From Bridge No. 12, near Spout Bank Farm, an excellent view could be had of the line between Heap Bridge Junction and Alfred Street bridge. Beyond the signal box were three sidings which, somewhat surprisingly, gave accommodation to 72 wagons when fully occupied. On this occasion we see a quantity of vans awaiting dispersal. Note the straight posted signal with its left hand "doll", normally found at the entrance to the loop rather than at a junction; in this case this signal controlled traffic which was about to leave the Up line and enter the Branch. Date and time: Saturday, 14th May 1966, at 09.30.

(Right) A WD 2-8-0 coasts downhill towards Bury past Heap Bridge Junction box with a westbound mixed freight. Note the sheeted five-plank wagons in the adjacent sidings. Winter 1960/61.   both: *Eric Bentley*

(Above) Now the site of Prettywood Garden Centre, this was the scene at Heap Bridge Goods at 09.30, Thursday, 3rd March 1966. Black 5 **44816** (Bolton shed), in a grimy condition, is spending some time on shunting duties in the cramped yard. To the left of the engine, a small coal concentration and distribution plant still provided local people and industries with vital fuel during the mid-1960s when open fires in houses and Lancashire boilers in industrial premises were the normal way of raising heat. The main traffic in the yard, apart from coal, were wood pulp for the local paper industry, and some chemicals. The sheeted wagons probably contained wood pulp and/or chemicals for Yates Duxbury, whose No.1 Mill lay nearby but off the photograph to the left. No.2 Mill stood behind the houses on Bury New Road, extreme left. To reach the goods yard, all rail traffic had to pass over a metal bridge spanning Heap Brow, the abutments of which are extant on either side of the narrow lane leading from Heap Bridge to Darn Hill, and Pilsworth.

(Right) Leaking steam badly, Black 5 **45202** (Newton Heath shed) storms the western entrance to Spout Bank Cutting with a five-coach train forming the 09.00 Liverpool Exchange to Rochdale express service. At 10.10, on Saturday, 11th March 1963, the photographer has caught the activity before being himself enshrouded in a cloud of smoke. Although not the most neatly-trimmed ballast, credit has to be awarded to the permanent way men whose responsibility it was to keep this section of line in apple-pie order. Keen-eyed readers will have noticed that the Up line consists of flat-bottomed rail, while the Down line remains the older type bull-head rail held in chairs by spring steel keys. *Both: Eric Bentley*

An east-bound freight train drawn by a work-stained Black Five No.**45018**, passes beneath Bridge No.10 crossed by Moss Hall Lane. The three-arched "Old Hands " bridge had spans of 30 feet between the piers on either side of the rails and was almost identical to Bridge No.11A, seen in the distance. Such structures were constructed by the Manchester & Leeds Railway Company during the extension of the railway from Heywood to Bury, which was opened for traffic by the LYR on the 1st May 1848. The extension was carried out under the supervision of John Hawkshaw, the M&L Chief Engineer, and built by the contractor George Thomson. These two bridges are extant and bear testimony to their design and construction after 150 years existence. Note the signal, mostly hidden by the sight-board.

Ray Farrell

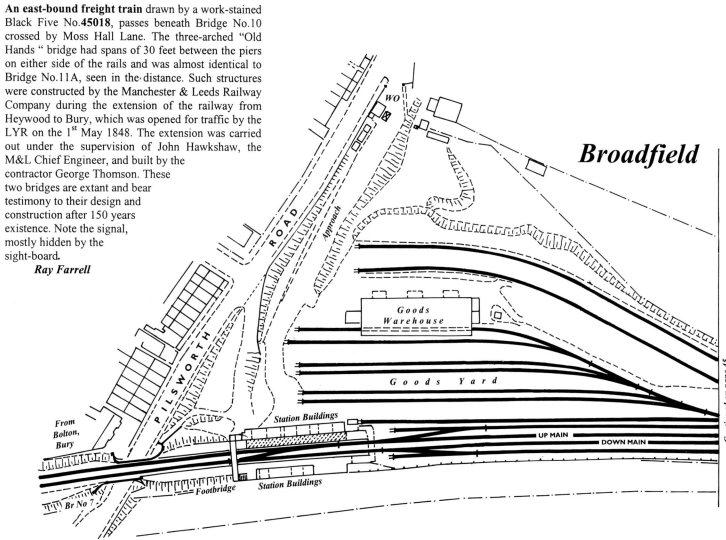

Broadfield

PILSWORTH

ROAD

Approach

WO

Goods Warehouse

Goods Yard

Station Buildings

From Bolton, Bury

Footbridge *Station Buildings*

Br No 7

UP MAIN   DOWN MAIN

Continued on page 45

Broadfield was never a popular spot with photographers and trainspotters. It was a fairly mundane location holding little of interest on the line between busy Bury and hectic Heywood. Not totally neglected, however, for our photographer has been tempted away from Bury and its locality to try his luck at Broadfield where, at 13.20, he has caught the 13.20Sx Rochdale to Liverpool Exchange service as it leaves Broadfield Station. The original station at Broadfield was of wooden construction, and suffered the ravages of a fire in the early morning of 3rd March 1883, being completely burnt down. A new station was built by the contractor Thomas Wrigley of Middleton Junction for about £11,000, opening in late 1883, to "consist of general, ladies and gentlemen's 1st Class waiting rooms, booking office, porters' room and lamp room, with similar buildings on the other [Down] platform." An impressive footbridge was erected in 1884 using wrought iron plate girders and a timber floor. As can be seen, passengers using it had the benefit of a half-glazed cover stretching from platform to platform. Thomas Wrigley junior's tender of £4,494.7.11 was recommended to be accepted for a new goods warehouse in June 1883. The result was a brick building similar in design to the larger version at Knowsley Street Goods, built on the northern side of a yard which could accommodate in the region of 195 wagons. A 1960s OS 25 inch plan shows extensive development on the south-eastern side of the station where two large loops were installed from which two sidings served a large warehouse comprising the Higher Broadfield Cold Storage Depot. The sidings lines in the foreground led into a set of five dead-end sidings to the west of Pilsworth Road.

Eric Bentley

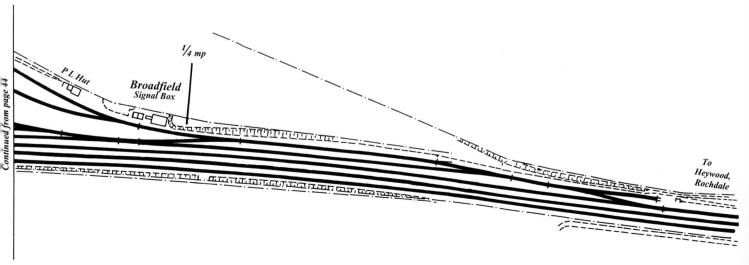

Continued from page 44

P L Hut

$^1/_4$ *mp*

Broadfield
Signal Box

To
Heywood,
Rochdale

Heywood

An interesting view from Manchester Street bridge, Heywood, taken on the 7th November 1964. Leaving the Down platform is a Metro Cammell 2-car Dmu bound, (if the indicator is to be believed) for Bacup, via Bury. Of a number of aspects of the station worth mentioning, the following are worth dwelling on. Beyond the stone retaining wall, is the the platform mounted banner repeater signal which showed drivers of Up trains the aspect of the Up platform starting signal obscured from view by the line's sharp curvature, the station footbridge, and the Down platform awnings. Close to the Up side station buildings is a LMS plate girder footbridge (Bridge No.2) erected in 1938 with a concrete floor. This was a replacement in the same position of an ornate LYR wrought iron lattice girder footbridge whose girders were strengthened in 1902. The cast iron columns erected on the platforms to support the bridge were retained. Note the platform garden boxes, neatly whitewashed to good effect, at the time tended regularly by station staff, and a source of pride. In an otherwise drab quarter of the town, pride there was in giving the station a modicum of colour, albeit only during the summer months. *Ray Farrell*

(Below) An unidentified member of one of Bolton's Stanier Class 4 "Big Tanks" awaits departure time with a westbound working from Rochdale. The overall journey times to Bolton fell within a nominal twenty five/thirty minute bracket, with a six minute schedule being the shortest time for the four miles to Bury Knowsley Street, inclusive of a stop at Broadfield. The "Rochdale to Bolton" service also enjoyed useful extensions to its itinerary of destinations, namely Blackpool (North and South), Southport, Liverpool Exchange, the latter pair of course including Wigan Wallgate. There was also an early morning Rochdale to Bacup train. *Eric Bentley*

From the Heywood Station footbridge, we glance down at two Rose Grove Black 5s drawing a train of ten carriages forming train number 1X05, the 08.21 Blackburn to Scarborough (via Bolton) Holiday Special. A few people await the special as it pulls into the station on a Saturday morning (09.21) on the 10th July 1965. Although car ownership was on the increase by the 1960s, travel by train over a distance of 50 miles or so was still preferable to going by A class roads, especially in those days before the advent of race-track motorways. Heywood Station was situated on a sharp curve in the line between Broadfield and Castleton - where the extension to Bury diverged from the original line from Castleton to a terminus station at Heywood - hence the need for check-rails on the inside of both curves. Perseverance Mill dominates the background, an ever-present reminder that holidays were only an ephemeral relief from the daily toil of thousands of Heywoodites.

Eric Bentley

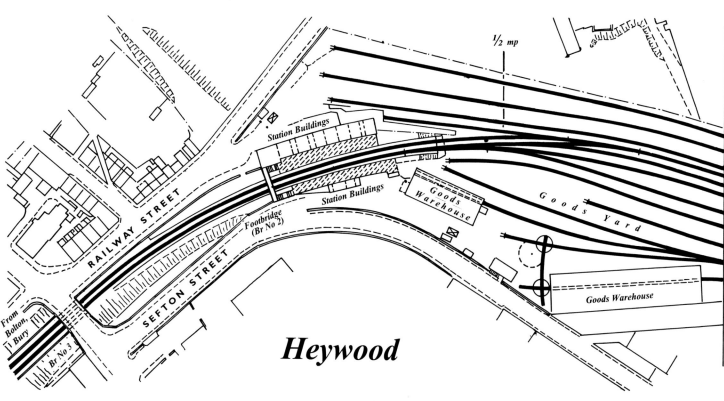

Heywood

(Left) The view from Green Lane footbridge, Heywood at 13.00, on a cold Friday, 22nd February 1963, looking towards the station. Stanier 8F **48139** (Widnes shed) has just passed beneath the footbridge, hauling a load of Yorkshire coal westwards. Heywood was not short of siding accommodation to serve the needs of the town; these were situated at the western end of the station, and can be seen in this view to be occupied by coal wagons, and a rake of ICI open wagons, possibly associated with the nearby Standard Railway Wagon Works. Far to the right is part of the end wall of the Perseverance Cotton Mill (built circa 1875) from which a loading hoist can be seen projecting over two doors. Note how the plain hexagonal chimney has been made higher by the brick stack added some time later. The former goods shed (the larger of the two) has been let for another's use, suggested by the word "machinists" portrayed on the wall. Centre stage is taken by two monuments to life in Heywood: Burns Cotton Mill chimney, representing toil, and St. Luke's Parish Church spire, representing man's spiritual needs. Previous snow-fall has thawed and then frozen in this dismal, wintry scene. *Eric Bentley*

The Scarborough Special has now reached a point just beyond Green Lane footbridge from which this view has been taken. A short time has elapsed so enabling the photographer to leave the station footbridge and take up a new position at Green Lane. Within an interval of fifteen minutes, the double-headed train will have arrived at Castleton and will have joined the Calder Valley line via Rochdale, Todmorden, Hebden Bridge, to Leeds. Approaching from the opposite direction is the 08.28 Brewery Sidings (Miles Platting) to Bury Knowsley Street goods, slowly taking the down gradient into Heywood. *Eric Bentley*

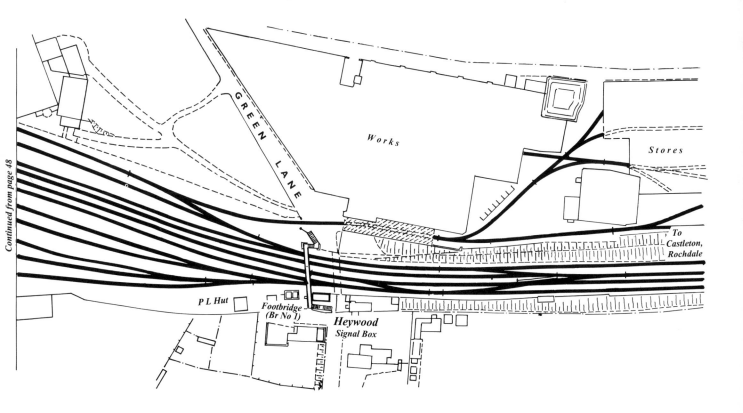

Continued from page 48

GREEN LANE

Works

Stores

To Castleton, Rochdale

P L Hut

Footbridge (Br No 1)

Heywood Signal Box

Westbound from Castleton. Stanier 8F **48139** (Widnes 8D) approaches Heywood with a west-bound mixed freight at 13.00, on Friday, 22nd February 1963. The four mile descent to Bury had begun at Castleton with a modest fall at 1 in 184. Cautious handling of brakes both at the front and rear of the train was needed before crews were faced with the tricky incline that was Broadfield bank, a two mile test of driving skills, particularly with a train fully loaded as this seen here. A scramble from rail level up the shallow bank on the left would bring you to the premises of the Standard Railway Wagon Company Ltd., previously the Lancashire & Yorkshire Waggon Company Ltd., and later to become Powell Duffryn. The Works had its own internal layout of sidings, the point of connection with the main line being at a trailing point a few yards west of Green Lane footbridge. Powell Duffryn took over the Standard R W Co. in 1989 and suffered a gradual decline in fortune thereafter. Fifty nine jobs were lost in December 1990, with short-time working introduced in July 1991. A further 43 jobs were lost in October 1991, all of these a consequence of the loss of orders. The firm called it a day at Christmas 1992, the remaining workforce of 53 being made redundant, the site once occupied by the firm now part of an industrial estate. The railway eastwards from this location maintained a gently curving course until it reached Castleton East Junction. Much of the coal traffic over this route was for railway use, particularly Liverpool area motive power depots. With the demise of steam, this useful link, providing what was very much a north Manchester-avoiding line, would be allowed to fade away.

Eric Bentley

Bury to Rawtenstall

PASSENGERS MUST CROSS THE LINE BY THE BRIDGE

The very heart of Bolton Street Station could arguably be taken to be beneath the pedestrian overbridge at the northern end of platform 3. At this point at 13.42, Saturday, 10th July 1965, an unidentified Black 5 assists **45338** (Llandudno shed) with train number 1C65, forming the 09.50 Llandudno to Manchester Victoria service, extended through to Ramsbottom. This was a scheduled summer service, extended beyond its usual destination for the benefit of Bury and Ramsbottom holiday makers. At Ramsbottom, the two engines ran round the empty train and returned as 3J87 with the empty stock tender first to Lightbowne Sidings, Moston, travelling via Knowsley Street, Castleton, Middleton Junction, and Newton Heath. The pilot engine from Newton Heath shed had assisted the train engine from Manchester Victoria. Both engines blow off as they approach the 80 yards long Bury EL Tunnel, on what appears to be a typically wet summer day. This close-up shot shows the disposition of the overbridge, erected in 1952, comprising brick stairwells and abutments with a reinforced concrete deck. The new structure replaced a platform overbridge which had consisted of wrought iron girders and timber flooring, supported on cast iron columns. Originally constructed in 1884 by the LYR, it was subsequently widened ten years later. The 1952 rebuild also replaced a booking hall which overspanned the lines. This comprised a stone arch with wrought iron main and cross girders with a timber floor, also constructed in 1884. Both booking hall and footbridge were connected by a covered passageway.

Eric Bentley

Bury Loco. On the 15th July 1964, when this evening photograph was taken, Bury engine shed (designated 9M in September 1961) was less than one year away from closure. It was in June 1875 that the Lancashire and Yorkshire Railway Company decided to erect an all-brick straight shed with a hipped roof, at a cost of £7,000. It opened the following year. In this view, two of the shed's eight roads are occupied by Crab **42831** (a Bury engine), and visiting Stanier 8F **48636** (9H, Patricroft). Far left stands Buckley Wells signal box strategically positioned to control Buckley Wells level crossing. Two fine examples of LMS semaphore signals graced this spot, both of which were balanced doll bracket types, one mounted on a tubular post, the other on a lattice post. Hiding from view the rear end of the Crab's tender is a Horwich-type water column, at the base of which lies an overturned fire-devil used in winter to counteract the effects of frost, but redundant during the summer months.

Steam Shed and "Car" Shops. Having moved towards the "Crab", the photographer now reveals a closer view of the southern aspect of the shed with its three hipped-roofed bays and turret-type roof venti-lators. Adjoining the shed was the electric car shop, part of the west-facing wall and roof appearing behind the Crab. Striking across the lower part of the photo-graph is a short section of the wooden cladding which protected the live pick-up rail used by the Manchester - Bury electric trains. The timber used for this purpose was Jarrah, an Australian hardwood which was regarded as fire-proof and durable. The cladding surrounded the live rails on three sides, leaving an internal vertical surface for the trains' contact shoes.

Both: Eric Bentley

Engines on shed. Three locomotives stand in line on the northern side of the once-familiar tank-over brick coal-hole (a relic L&Y feature), at 20.30, Thursday, 27th June 1957. A rather smart Ivatt 2-6-0, No. **46406** portrays an early British Railways emblem on its lined tender; in front are two Stanier 4MT 2-6-4s, No. **42455** and another unfortunately unidentifiable. The brick coal stage or coal-hole was built to accommodate three or four wagons loaded with coal which were propelled up a ramp on to a level platform from which the coal was tipped and shovelled into waiting tenders and bunkers. Bury shed (26D in 1957) never boasted a cenotaph coaling plant, having instead to make do with this earlier form of coaling facility. As has been commented elsewhere, *"the coal stages were no havens of rest, involving hard manual labour in arduous conditions"* (LMS Engine Sheds Vol.3) Dozens of Bury men who worked in the stage would no doubt have agreed with this statement.

Nocturnal Bury. Light streams through the windows of the electric car shop, indicative that the night shift is underway at 22.05, Sunday, 27th October 1957. Outside, the light of a single yard lamp throws an Ivatt 2-6-0 and a 2-6-4 tank engine into a hazy silhouette.

A blaze of light emanates from the interior of Bury shed when this photograph was taken in early 1958. Standing inside is an Austerity 2-8-0, its funnel belching smoke, and safety valves in full throttle. The tender of a sister engine stands in front, whilst the front end of a Fowler 4F pauses before a yard signal whose bent ladder rises to the top of the post from ground level. The long time exposure for this photograph shows the effects of wind on the plume of smoke which rapidly disperses after leaving the roof ventilators. Shed employees worked in an ambience of smoke, steam, wet, and noise. It was the combination of these which made the job unique. *Eric Bentley (3)*

Bury Shed, 26 October 1957. Reference to my Ian Allan's ABC "British Railways Locomotives" (Summer 1955 edition) furnishes the following concise description of the Crab locomotive: "Introduced 1926. Hughes LMS design built under Fowler's direction. Walschaert's Valve Gear. P.V. Weight: Loco 66 tons 0 cwt. Pressure: 180lbs Su [Superheated]. Cyls: O [Outside] 21 ins x 26 ins. Dr. Wheels: 5 ft 6 ins. T.E. [Tractive Effort] 26,580lbs". Here we see one of the 245 Crabs built for the LMS, standing outside Bury shed, a fine example of Horwich engineering, and by this date, thirty years old. With a 5MT classification, the Crabs were at home with both freight and passenger traffic, a versatility often displayed during the 1950s when Jeffrey Wells was a keen trainspotter.

Eric Bentley

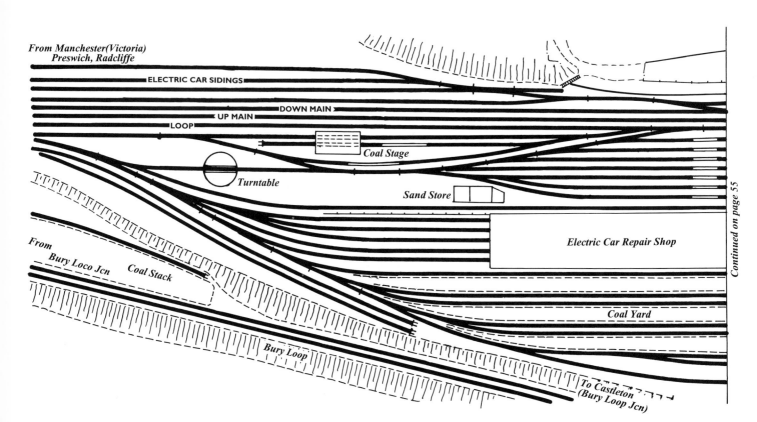

Continued on page 55

The approach from Manchester, via Prestwich, towards Bolton Street, is framed in this view by the locally known "Victoria" footbridge; this was originally built of timber beams and decking and was lengthened in 1894. The middle span (40ft 9ins), was reconstructed with steel joists bearing a reinforced concrete floor in 1938, whilst a shorter 10ft 6ins span was also renewed in the same year with timber beams and decking. Through the left hand opening can be seen the roof outline of Bury MPD. Buckley Wells signal box is to the right of the bridge pier.

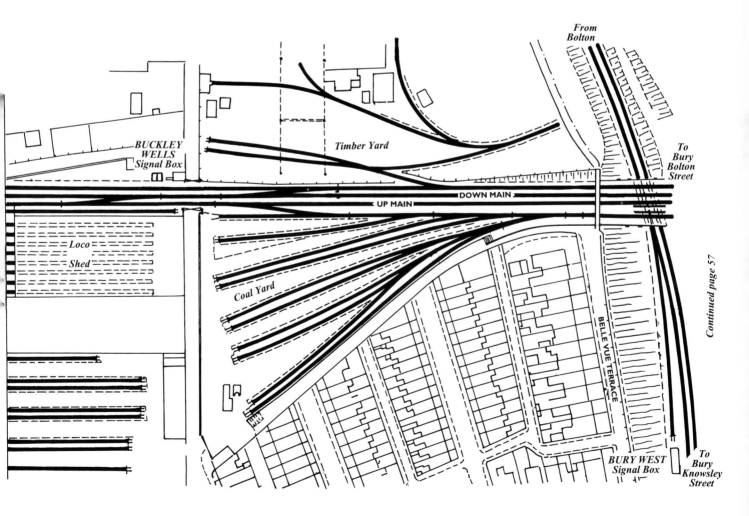

Continued page 57

From the elevated position of footbridge No.25 near to Belle Vue Terrace on a damp and dreary summer's day, we obtain this view towards Bolton Street Station which is just visible beyond Tenterden Street bridge. Approaching the station is a pair of Stanier Black Fives, **45311** (Llandudno Junction) the train engine, with train number 1C64, the 09.25 Caernarvon to Manchester Exchange service, extended to Ramsbottom. At "Rammy", the locomotives ran round their train and returned as 3J87 (the general reporting number for Lightbowne Carriage Sidings, Moston) tender first via Castleton. The extended service to Ramsbottom occurred once a year during the Bury and district holidays. Bury South signal box (LYR 311) of 1910 vintage occupied a site wedged between the Up main line and the Up goods loop from which Angle Sidings fanned out. Engineering work took place at the location of the bridge over the Bolton to Rochdale line during September and October 1965 in which the bridge decking, parapet, and track work were substantially altered. This underbridge was classed as an intersection type; it had square span of 27ft 6ins; 28 ft 9ins skew span with steel girders and steel plated parapets resting on stone abutments. It was constructed in 1895 to carry the Up and Down main lines, Down goods line, and Up Loop line.

A Metro Cammell two-car Dmu, sporting its high-visibility "speed-whiskers", stands in the Up Loop whilst a double-headed holiday special thunders past on Saturday, 1st July 1961. A Rose Grove Black 5, **45229** and an unidentified sister engine draw the holiday train out of Bolton Street Station on the first leg of the journey to North Wales. In this view, smoke partly obscures the right-hand bracket which holds colour light signals. Despite inquiries, it has not been fully established when these colour searchlight signals were first installed at Bury, but current thinking fixes the 1930s as being most probable. *Eric Bentley (2)*

"Bury's" Crab, 42700 seen here in its active BR days, on Saturday, 6th July 1963, pulling a Bury holiday special to Liverpool Exchange (the L&Y's station at Liverpool) for a connection with ferries to the Isle of Man. The view has been taken from Tenterden Street bridge at the early hour of 06.45. The special had started at Ramsbottom, stopped to pick up at Summerseat and Bury, and will take the Bolton line at Radcliffe, thence proceeding via Bradley Fold and Bolton. The East Fork (with check rails) can be seen sloping down gradient towards Knowsley Street Station to the left of the engine. The three-span "Victoria" footbridge, illustrated on page 55, crosses the line beyond the signal box. The Down Slow line on the far right became the Down Siding in late 1965 and was provided with a stop-block 10 yards on the north side of the intersection bridge, just beyond the colour light bracket signal. A fine length of point rodding lies adjacent to the signal box, while Angle Sidings are noticeably deserted. Following a long association with Bury, 42700 left in the autumn of 1964, initially for a short spell at Gorton. This was followed by a move to Buxton, the locomotive's penultimate base before withdrawal in March 1966 whilst at Birkenhead. Earmarked for preservation, the engine was put into store and subsequently displayed at the National Railway Museum. In recent years however, due to pressure on space at the NRM, 42700 has been in store at Bury. Further re-location has seen the loco transferred in an unrestored condition to the Barrow Hill steam shed project.

Eric Bentley

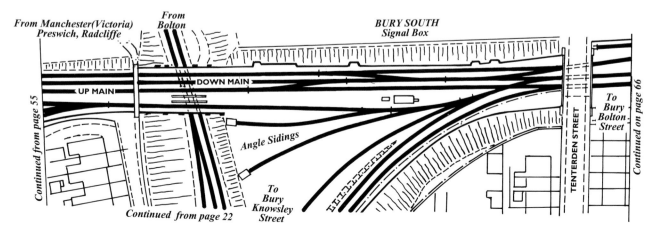

BRITISH RAILWAYS

THE WEST OF ENGLAND
Friday Night 5th July
LIGHT REFRESHMENTS WILL BE AVAILABLE ON THESE TRAINS

FROM			DEPARTURE TIMES		
	Schedule No.		150 p m †	151 p m †	152 p m †
Ramsbottom	...	...	7 § 32	8 32	
Summerseat	...	...	7 § 37	8 37	
Bury Bolton Street	...	...	7 § 40	8 44	10
Radcliffe Bridge	...	...	8 § 0	—	10 11
			am	am	a m
Bristol Temple Meads	...	...	—	2T 51	4T 12
Weston-Super-Mare	...	...	—	3A 40	6A 56
Bridgwater	...	...	—	4A 12	7A 30
Taunton	...	...	3T 0	4T 3	5T 29
Barnstaple Victoria Road	...	...	—	6B 52	8B 42
Braunton	...	...	—	7B 45	9B 27
Dulverton	...	...	—	6B 5	7B 45
Ilfracombe	...	...	—	8B 14	9B 58
Minehead	...	...	—	7B 55	7B 55
Mortehoe	...	...	—	8B 5	9B 45
South Molton	...	...	—	6B 30	8B 18
Watchet	...	...	—	7B 31	7B 31
Wellington	...	...	—	7B 42	7B 42
Tiverton	...	...	—	—	8C 22
Exeter St. Davids	...	...	3T 40	4T 48	6T 11
Dawlish	...	...	—	5D 55	7D 8
Teignmouth	...	...	—	5T 14	6T 36
Newton Abbot	...	...	4T 15	5T 25	6T 47
Torre	...	...	—	5T 49	7T 5
Torquay	...	...	—	5T 59	7T 19
Paignton	...	...	—	7E 10	7T 19
Churston	...	...	—	7F 42	8E 22
Brixham	...	...	—	7E 24	8F 32
Kingswear	...	...	5T 20		8E 35
Plymouth North Road	...	...	6G 29		
Saltash	...	...	6 T30		
Liskeard	...	...			
Bodmin Road	...	...	6T 48		
Par	...	...	7T 6		
Truro	...	...	8H 40		
Falmouth	...	...	9J 40		
Newquay	...	...	8T 49		
Helston	...	...	10K 44		
St. Ives	...	...	10L 34		
Penzance	...	...	9H 50		

Late in the evening (22.55) of Friday, 2nd July 1965, Black 5 **44817** (Agecroft shed) is set to leave platform 3 at Bolton Street Station as train number 1V82, the 23.23 Manchester Victoria to Paignton. Before its arrival at Bury, the train had started its journey at Burnley to cater for Rossendale holidays. The overnight journey would have conveyed many holiday makers who dozed off where they sat, without the comfort of beds. From my own experience, this kind of lengthy overnight journey was undertaken in the 1950s without trepidation, for it permitted a week or a fortnight's holiday on the Devon Riviera (Tor Bay), the place to go to see the sun before the advent of holidays in Ibiza and Majorca. Long before the availability of privately-owned cars, and motorways to run them on, journey by rail to the South West was the only sensible way to travel. As a boy trainspotter, the journey by night was long and tedious; far better to travel by day when it was possible to stand for hours on end in a side corridor, with notebook and pen at the ready to jot down hundreds of loco numbers, disrupted by the absolute necessity of snatching a meal and visits to the toilet. Details of the corresponding trains for 1957 are detailed in the handbill.   *Eric Bentley*

Austerity 90226 heads back to Bury shed tender first, and is about to pass beneath Tenterden Street bridge. The photograph has been taken from above the stone retaining wall which overlooks the eastern side of the station, and from this vantage point we can obtain a clear view of the railway-owned footpath bounded by the iron fence, plus the cast iron segmental girders and plates of bridge No.27 which had a span of 70 feet 4 ins. Beyond the bridge lie the start of the curved lines forming East Fork disappearing to the left out of view. This is a scene with a difference since most photographs show views of the station rather than its western end. At the end of platforms 3 and 4, above the ramp, is a colour light signal which read from Platform 4 to Up Main & Down Slow. Following the truncation of the latter, the signal referred to movements to the Down Siding only. The date of the photograph is 5th June 1963.

Eric Bentley

Bury's "premier" station enjoys a quiet period on Saturday, 29th February 1964. The absence of trains allows the reader's eye to wander over the station and absorb the details which are often obscured by engines, smoke, and steam. The prosaic canopy over platforms 3 and 4 was supported on original LYR cast iron columns and superstructure, and extended some 380 feet from the 1953-built pedestrian link bridge, comfortably sheltering all the Down side buildings. The cast iron posts are wider apart than those on platforms 1 and 2 in order to accommodate these buildings. The ground floor of the old ELR headquarters housed the Up side facilities, the canopies over the Up side extending the complete length of the building, and over the platforms beyond. Behind platform 4, at the top of a shallow cutting stood the ex-LYR brick, tank-over water tower which supplied the station and locomotives with a good head of water, fed at on time from the nearby Elton reservoir. Readers with long memories will recognise the large building with a pitched roof which overlooked the northern end of the station. This had been a pre-war cinema, which assumed a new role after the war by becoming the town's "Palais de Dance", where later, scores of "Teddy boys" in suede shoes or "winkle-pickers" gathered in order to gyrate to the sounds of the day. In its day, the Palais had hosted Julie Goodyear (ex-Coronation Street) who experienced being the target for missiles during one of her performances. The Palais burned down in 1970, taking its memories up in smoke.

Ray Farrell

A 4F 0-6-0, No 44567 runs light engine on the Down line at the southern end of Bolton Street Station. From the vantage point afforded by Tenterden Street bridge, the photographer has been able to portray the station to full effect and this is how it looked on the 29th February 1964. The arrangement of semaphores deserves explanation. Those mounted on the balanced two-doll bracket signals (far right) controlled movements from Bay Platform 1, the taller arms for departures to Radcliffe, the lower for those to Knowsley Street. The right-hand bracket at the end of platform 2 performed a similar function. At the southern end of platform 3, a single post carries four subsidiary signal arms reading, from top to bottom, to Knowsley Street, Angle Siding, Up Main & Down Slow(Bang Road). Far left was an early colour light signal which controlled departures from platform 4 to Up Main & Down Slow. *Ray Farrell*

(Below-left) This view was taken on the 10th April 1971 and shows the changes which have taken place at Bolton Street Station. Gone is the canopy over platforms 1 and 2, except for a fragment which has survived at the northern-most end. Gone too is most of the canopy over platforms 3 and 4; much of the original has been cut back and partly rebuilt at the northern end, a portion of which remains today. Changes have taken place with respect to the tall signal post at the Manchester end of platforms 3 and 4. In place of four short arms, which were later reduced to three, the signal post has normal size stop and distant arms and a remaining short arm. The Section C Notices for the 10th to 24th April 1970 reveal all: *"The three armed straight post signal situated at the Manchester end of Bury Station Up and Down fast platform and applying to the Up connecting line or Angle Sidings or Up Main will be replaced by a new straight post signal in the same position. This signal will have a main arm 25 feet above rail level applying to the Up Main or Up connecting line and will have a 2-way stencil type route indicator [not installed in the photograph] associated with it displaying M or C respectively when the signal is cleared. Beneath it will be a distant arm which, when applying to the Up Main, will be 365 yards to Buckley Wells Up Main home signal, and when applying to the Up connecting line, will be 238 yards to Bury Knowsley Street Up connecting line to the Angle Sidings. A subsidiary signal arm will be provided applying to the Angle Sidings".* The signal post also received a diamond sign to denote that it was exempt from Rule 55. Standing on the Down line alongside platform 2 is an English Electric Type 4, later to become Class 40, with its train of "Manchester Explorer Rail Tour" enthusiasts. *Ray Farrell*

Bolton Street Station on a showery Sunday morning, 5th May 1963. From Tenterden Street bridge (No.27) a superb view of the station unfolded, and on that particular day, the station was far from being at its busiest. In the bay, alongside platform 1, a lone electric car set awaits departure, one of those making up the half-hourly service to Manchester on Sundays. In 1963, most of the fabric of the station was untouched; the ELR headquarters still maintains a presence overlooking the station; the cluster of buildings which still stand on the Down platform find protection beneath a well-maintained canopy; overlooking platform 4 stands the LYR brick, tank-over water tower which supplied the station with copious amounts of water; and to grace the scene are three examples of semaphore signals. The track work is ostensibly in good order as are the well-swept, litter-free platforms. Between the railings and the sturdy stone retaining wall lay a footpath which led back to Knowsley Street Station, skirting the East Fork, a path upon which hundreds of railway personnel walked over the years.

Eric Bentley

(Right-lower) The Manchester end of Bolton Street Station was dominated by the two sets of bracketed semaphore signals. Signalling enthusiasts have, in this photograph, the opportunity to focus their attention on the rear side of those in the foreground thus obtaining some idea of the detailing of them. Standing on the tiny wooden platform on a wet and windy day must have daunted all but the boldest heart, especially when it was necessary to mount one or other of the ladders to reach the lamps. Standing at platform 4 is one of the green liveried Wolverton-built Emu sets which has either just arrived from Manchester, or is about to set off on the return journey.

Ray Farrell

(Right) The sight of this illuminated display suspended from the platform roofing greeted passengers circulating on platforms 3 & 4. Possibly of L&Y origin, most certainly containing features associated with Horwich, this indicator displayed times and destinations for the services using these two platforms. By this time the Holcombe Brook service had ended but there was still extensive usage by trains to and from East Lancashire. The time and platform of the next electric service direct to Manchester Victoria via Prestwich was indicated in the central display. It was operated electrically from an office on the platform. 24th February 1954.

(Below) Bolton Street Station, looking north from platform 3. At first sight, the year could be 1920, and the belief could be entertained that a train entering the station from Accrington or Bacup in the shape of an LYR Aspinall 0-6-0, or a Tottington Branch Emu, might appear at any moment. The date is, in fact, Thursday, 26th October 1950. The giveaway is the carriage at the bay platform, portraying the logo "British Railways", and also the poster on the wall announcing the Daily Telegraph's "Latest News from Korea", a war which had begun in the June of that year in a country few had ever heard of. Apart from these details, the station is much as it would have been in those "Business Line" days which ended in 1923, the influence of which was to continue to haunt the LMS for many years. It is possible to see the LYR footbridge and the covered platform approach leading to it from the booking hall. Both were constructed in 1884 using masonry, wrought iron, and timber. Both were to be consumed by fire on the 17th May 1947. Close scrutiny of the window to the rear of the booking hall reveals jagged shards of glass in the frame, the result, no doubt, from the fire and the assault on it by the fire brigade. Back on platform 3 other contemporary posters characterise the 1950s - "Germolene" was the answer to cuts and bruises, whilst the Daily Telegraph was running Winston Churchill's Memoirs, his war time premiership still fresh in people's minds. *BR(LMR)*

Special Excursion

BY

DIESEL TRAIN

SKIPTON   BOLTON ABBEY
ILKLEY

SUNDAY 20th JULY 1958

FROM	Departure Times	RETURN FARES - SECOND CLASS			Arrival Times On Return
		Skipton	Bolton Abbey	Ilkley	
	a.m.	s. d.	s. d.	s. d.	p.m.
ROCHDALE	11 5	6/3	7/3	7/9	9 10
CASTLETON	11 10	6/3	7/3	7/6	9 6
HEYWOOD	11 15	6/-	6/9	7/-	8 55
BURY Bolton Street	11 28	5/9	6/6	6/3	8 36
HELMSHORE	11 44	4/6	5/9	5/9	8 26
ACCRINGTON	11 55	3/9	3/9	4/3	7 55
BURNLEY Central	12 9	3/-	3/9	3/9	7 41
NELSON	12 18	2/9	3/3	3/3	
ARRIVAL TIMES		p.m. 12 35	p.m. 12 55	p.m. 1 5	
RETURN TIMES		p.m. 7 25	p.m. 7 10	p.m. 7 0	

SPECIAL NOTICE

Tickets for this Excursion will be Strictly Limited to the seating capacity of the tra
Passengers are requested to Book their Tickets in Advance.

Children under three years of age free; three and under fourteen years of age, half-
These tickets are issued subject to British Transport Commission's published Reg
and Conditions applicable to British Railways exhibited at their Stations or obtainable free o
at Station Booking Offices.
TICKETS CAN BE OBTAINED IN ADVANCE AT THE STATIONS AND OFFICIAL RAIL
AGENTS

Further information will be supplied on application to the Stations, Official Railway A
to Mr. T. W. POLDING, District Passenger Manager, L.M.R., Hunts Bank, Manchester, 3.
3456, Ext. 382.

June, 1959   XA/HD

LONDON MIDLAND

Hills Printers, Chorley.

Organised Rambles
FROM

GRASSINGTON

(FOR ROUTES SEE OVER)

RAMBLES AVAILABLE FOR INDIVIDUALS AS
WELL AS ORGANISED PARTIES

LEADERS PROVIDED

Special Excursion
BURNLEY NELSON COLNE SKIPTON
GRASSINGTON

SUNDAY 30th AUGUST 1959

FROM	Dep. Times	RETURN FARES Second Class					Return Arrival Times
		Burnley Central	Nelson	Colne	Skipton	Grass-ington	
	a.m.	s. d.	s. d.	s. d.	s. d.	s. d.	p.m.
MANCHESTER (Victoria)	10 15	4 6	4 6	3 5	5 9	8 3	9 26
BURY (Bolton Street)	10 40	3 6	3 6	3 9	5 9	7 3	9 5
HELMSHORE	10 55	2 0	2 6	3 0	4 6	6 9	8 51
ACCRINGTON	11 10	—	—	—	3 9	6 6	8 32
ROSE GROVE	11 20	—	—	—	3 3	5 3	8 23
BURNLEY (Barracks)	11 25	—	—	—	3 0	5 3	8 18
BURNLEY (Central)	11 30	—	—	—	3 0	5 3	8 15
BRIERFIELD	11 40	—	—	—	3 0	5 0	8 4
NELSON	11 45	—	—	—	—	4 6	8 0
COLNE	11 50	—	—	—	—	4 6	7 54
EARBY	11 59	—	—	—	—	3 3	7 43
SKIPTON	p.m. 12 15	—	—	—	—	2 0	7 30
ARRIVAL TIMES		a.m. 11 30	a.m. 11 45	a.m. 11 50	p.m. 12 15	p.m. 12 43	
RETURN TIMES		p.m. 8 15	p.m. 8 0	p.m. 7 54	p.m. 7 30	p.m. 7 0	

Children under three years of age, free; three and under fourteen years of age, half-fare.
CONDITIONS OF ISSUE OF EXCURSION AND OTHER TICKETS AT LESS THAN ORDINARY FARES
These tickets are issued subject to the British Transport Commission's published Regulations
and Conditions applicable to British Railways exhibited at their Stations or obtainable free of charge
at Station Booking Offices.
TICKETS CAN BE OBTAINED IN ADVANCE AT THE STATIONS AND OFFICIAL RAILWAY
AGENTS
Further information will be supplied on application to the Stations, Official Railway Agents, or
to Mr. T. W. POLDING, District Passenger Manager, L.M.R., Hunts Bank, Manchester, 3. Tel. BLA
3456, Ext. 382.

August 1959   XB/HD   PLEASE SEE OVER

LONDON MIDLAND

Hills Printers, Chorley.   BR 35001   E 820/HD

A busy scene at Bolton Street, on Sunday, 29th September 1957. The permanent way gang has spent the day re-ballasting the lines through the station. The driver of a Black 5 looks on as his train from Colne departs on the journey via Clifton Junction for Manchester Victoria. Working under possession in platform 3 (bi-directional) is an unidentified Crab at the head of an engineers ballast train. Time is getting on; the "gaffer", with collar and tie, probably the Permanent Way Inspector, looks at his watch - it is already 16.20, and the work not yet completed. No.1 bay platform plays host to a 5-car ex-LYR electric multiple set, revolutionary in design when introduced in 1916, but, according to those who travelled by them, bone-shakers by the 1950s. This was the fascination of the station: the unusual blend of steam, diesel, and electric traction present at one location. The residents of the houses on the other side of the retaining wall had an excellent vantage point to witness the goings-on at the station, but, as in many cases of familiarity, were probably nonchalant about the ever-changing scene at Bury's premier station.
Eric Bentley

An unusual occurrence at Bolton Street was the visit of a Western Pullman, 8-car set on Saturday, 28th January 1967. This was one of three specials which ran to the station on the occasion of Bury FC's cup-tie with Walsall FC, a game which was won by Bury two goals to nil, before a crowd of 14,244 at Gigg Lane. The Pullmans were introduced by BR in 1959, dazzling everyone with their 1,000 h.p. engines at each end, along with their sleek styling. Five sets were built by Metro Cammel: two, 6-car sets for the Midland Region's Manchester to St. Pancras service, and three, 8-car sets for the Western Region to run between Paddington, Bristol, and Birmingham. Despite their smart appearance all suffered from poor riding and persistent vibration. In this photograph, the Western Pullman awaits departure with train number 1Z65 from Bury on the return journey to the Black Country. The two other visiting specials to Bury that day were electrically hauled to Stockport Edgeley, and brought to Knowsley Street Station by Black 5s. These ran from Stockport via Denton Junction, Droylsden Station Junction, Philips Park, Brewery Sidings, and Castleton. *Eric Bentley*

Enthusiasts armed with cameras gathered on platforms 3 and 4 on the occasion of the "Three Counties" tour which began at Bury and ran via Clifton Junction, Manchester Victoria, Denton Junction, to Stockport. The scene is caught at 12.45, Saturday, 26th November 1966 as two "Jinties" (9D, Newton Heath shed), Nos. **47383** and condensing type **47202** are fired up ready for departure. 47202 was one of the original 29 of the class built in 1899 to a Johnson Midland design, rebuilt in 1919. Seventeen of the 29 were condensing locomotives distinguished by the large diameter pipes on either side of the boiler from the smokebox to the side tanks. Only two of this class had survived by 1966, the other engine based at Patricroft shed. No. 47383 was one of 369 built by the LMS and introduced in 1924. *Eric Bentley*

A "proceed with caution" has been given to the 09.10 (Sx) Colne to Manchester Victoria semi-fast as it passes Bolton Street Station on Wednesday, 14th August 1963. The train ran non-stop from Helmshore to Salford, taking a journey time of 25 minutes. The engine, a Stanier 4MT, **42640**, had earlier worked the 05.14 Manchester Victoria to Colne parcels train on the same day. In No.1 platform, a Wolverton stock Emu awaits departure for Manchester Victoria. Strangely, the station appears to be devoid of people, unusual for a midweek morning.

Eric Bentley

The erstwhile headquarters of the East Lancashire Railway latterly provided accommodation for a multiplicity of administrative functions, not least the District Permanent Way Inspector and his staff. This October 1950 view shows the elevation fronting platform 2 looking in the direction of Manchester. *British Railways(LMR)*

At 12.45, Monday, 20th September 1965, Black 5, **45258** of Bolton shed, steams into the station with a Knowsley Street to Blackpool half-day Illuminations excursion, a highlight for many who took advantage of the Bury September break. A group of people awaits the arrival of the train with anticipation of the day ahead, for the sun is shining and Blackpool is but two hours away. At platform 4, a 1959 Wolverton-built electric multiple train stands ready for its return trip to Manchester. Note the third-class non-corridor stock of the excursion train, complete with slam doors, footboards, and windows to hang out of during the journey. By using the telephoto lens, the photographer has brought the station and its immediate surroundings closer for our scrutiny and enjoyment.

Eric Bentley

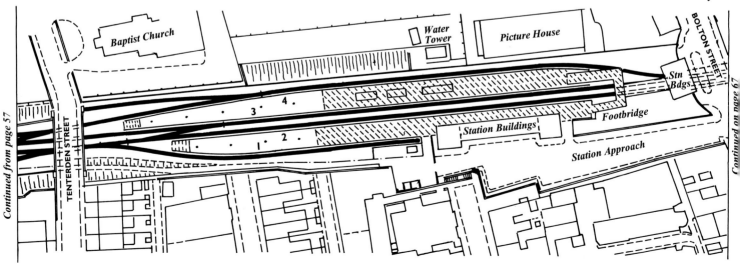

Continued from page 57

Continued on page 67

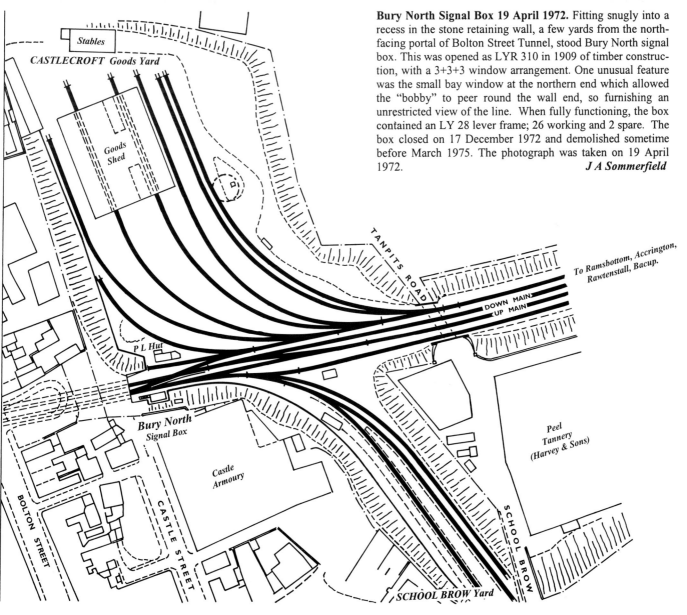

Bury North Signal Box 19 April 1972. Fitting snugly into a recess in the stone retaining wall, a few yards from the north-facing portal of Bolton Street Tunnel, stood Bury North signal box. This was opened as LYR 310 in 1909 of timber construction, with a 3+3+3 window arrangement. One unusual feature was the small bay window at the northern end which allowed the "bobby" to peer round the wall end, so furnishing an unrestricted view of the line. When fully functioning, the box contained an LY 28 lever frame; 26 working and 2 spare. The box closed on 17 December 1972 and demolished sometime before March 1975. The photograph was taken on 19 April 1972. *J A Sommerfield*

Stables

CASTLECROFT Goods Yard

Goods Shed

P L Hut

Bury North Signal Box

Castle Armoury

TANPITS ROAD

To Ramsbottom, Accrington, Rawtenstall, Bacup.

DOWN MAIN
UP MAIN

Peel Tannery (Harvey & Sons)

BOLTON STREET

CASTLE STREET

SCHOOL BROW

SCHOOL BROW Yard

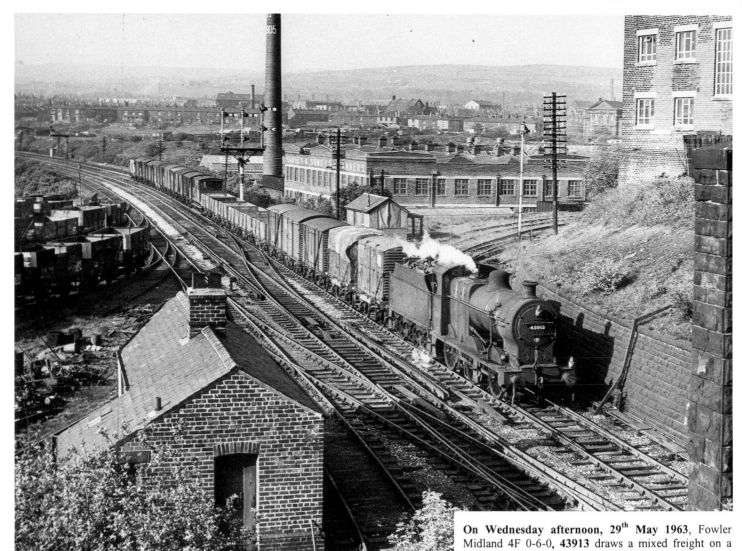

On Wednesday afternoon, 29th May 1963, Fowler Midland 4F 0-6-0, **43913** draws a mixed freight on a Bacup to Moston Sidings working. The first two wagons are Conflats, forming part of the Speedfreight service which was the forerunner of the BR Freightliner service introduced in 1964/5. The train is about to pass Bury North signal box, which occupied a recess in the retaining wall, and enter the 80 yards long Bury EL Tunnel. School Brow Coal Sidings, seen curving away to the right, behind the engine, had a capacity for 47 wagons; they now look neglected and unused. Castlecroft (or Bury Bolton Street Yard) was, on this day, replete with empty coal wagons. According to officialdom, *"Consideration is being given to the closure of Bury (EL) goods yard at which point only a very small amount of goods traffic will remain to be dealt with as the largest user - Messrs Harvey's Tanneries - are to concentrate their activities at their Nantwich Works"*. The goods yard closed, in fact, on the 7th October 1963, along with School Brow Coal Sidings. Harvey's chimney proclaims to all the origin of the modern works, although the business had been the three Harvey brothers' hands since 1870.

Ex-LYR 0-6-0 52523 of Bolton shed ambles towards Bury EL Tunnel with a five-coach train with the "Roch Valley Railway Society" special after taking the train from Tottington Junction to Bacup. Here we see the train on its return journey. The LMS tubular balanced doll bracket signal indicates that it will take the East Fork after leaving Bolton Street Station en route to Rochdale via Heywood and Castleton. The railtour took place on Saturday, 28th July 1962.   *Eric Bentley (2)*

We take our leave of Bolton Street and the local area with this view of a 2-6-4T heading north with the non-stop 16.20 Manchester Victoria to Colne express, that is, non-stop between Salford and Accrington. This service was the successor to the well-known 16.25 Salford to Colne express and was photographed at 16.40 on Friday, 2nd June 1961. On every scene taken of the railway north of Bury EL Tunnel, we have seen School Brow Sidings in a defunct state; only Castlecroft Yard appears, on this occasion, to be in use with a complement of wagons, two of which are sheeted. Forming the immediate background is an expanse of terraced housing which occupied the inner built-up area of northern Bury, backed by the subdued relief of the hills of southern Rossendale.

A run-of-the-mill scene north of Bury EL Tunnel at 18.30, Wednesday, 29th May 1963. Stanier 8F **48437** (Stockport Edgeley shed) draws a train of vans into Bury, a thin wisp of steam escaping from the safety valves. This train formed the 17.15 Nelson to Moston Sidings Class D goods. Like the Austerity class locomotives, the Stanier 8Fs were ubiquitous, more usually found hauling goods trains, but it was not surprising to see them working passenger trains when a shortage of more suitable motive power meant the deployment of these work horses. The signal cleared on the balanced signal bracket permits the train to continue towards the East Fork on its journey via Heywood and Castleton.   Both: *Eric Bentley*

Escaping steam rises skywards from 0-6-0 3F **47584** (Bury shed) as she toils bunker first up the gradient of 1 in 377, over the bridge (No 31) spanning Tanpits Road, towards Tottington Junction, on a murky Friday morning at 08.30, Monday, 12th May 1961. In tow are three 16 ton steel mineral wagons, followed by a number of 5-plank general merchandise wagons, and a lone ICI 20 ton rail tank. Across the railway, despite the poor visibility, it is possible to discern the low-lying land known as Bury Ground over which the river Irwell flows. In the foreground are the redundant rails of School Brow Sidings, and part of the single storey buildings of Harvey's Tannery.
Eric Bentley

With Harvey's Tannery to his left - out of the picture - the photographer stands amongst the track side jungle of bushes and rose-bay willow herb, with his camera pointing south west towards Castlecroft Goods Yard. Caught on film is a "double-header" travelling north out of Bury, with a Radcliffe to Bridlington/Filey/Scarborough holiday special. The train is being drawn by an unidentified Crab piloting an equally unidentifiable Jubilee. It is a matter of speculation as to which route the train will take beyond Accrington, one possible route being via Burnley, Colne, and into Yorkshire via Skipton, or by way of Copy Pit, Todmorden, and Leeds. Of the holiday makers on board, a good number will have Butlin's Holiday Camp as their final destination. The photograph was taken at 08.05, Saturday, 3rd July 1965.
Eric Bentley

Caught by the camera for posterity at 11.09, on Saturday, 26th November 1966, the "Three Counties Tour" sets forth with train number 1T55, the 10.00 Manchester Victoria to Bury and Bacup, a special organised by the Manchester Rail Travel Society. Upon returning to Manchester, thence to Stockport, it then travelled to Buxton. The view shows the train which has just passed over the bridge spanning Tanpits Road, shortly before reaching Tottington Junction. An industrialised scene forms the backcloth to the railway at this point, dominated by Chamber Hall Electricity Works with its four steel chimneys, and seen here in a derelict condition. Supply of electricity in Bury dates from 5th November 1898, and with increasing demand, a new electricity works at Chamber Hall was selected, generating power for the first time on 28th August 1911. It was reported in 1912 that the Works had its own sidings into which coal wagons were hauled by an electric capstan, the coal being fed into hoppers below the tracks. Ash and cinders were brought up to the sidings by hoists and dropped into the same wagons which had brought the coal. Water was drawn from the Irwell at Summerseat, and conveyed to the works by gravity via a goyt. A tablet on the north wall of the works read: "Upon this spot stood Chamber Hall, the birthplace of Sir Robert Peel, Baronet, Born 5th February 1788; Twice Prime Minister. Died 2nd July 1850." *Eric Bentley*

Railway interest takes a back seat in this photograph, the chief features of the scene being the disposition of Harvey's tannery works, the ringed chimney taking centre stage, with the wooden cooling towers of Chamber Hall Electricity Works (left), the four steel chimneys of the Works - originally there was a single brick chimney, extant in 1957; and beyond, the unmistakable Lancashire edifice devoted to cotton spinning, in the shape of Peel Mills. Small by comparison is Tottington Junction signal box (far right), establishing the position of the railway north of Bury. Careful scrutiny will also reveal sets of semaphore signals, and wagon ends marking the position of part of Tottington Branch Sidings. A thin veneer of snow picks out mounds of coal forming the Electricity Works' stocks.
Eric Bentley

Tottington Junction

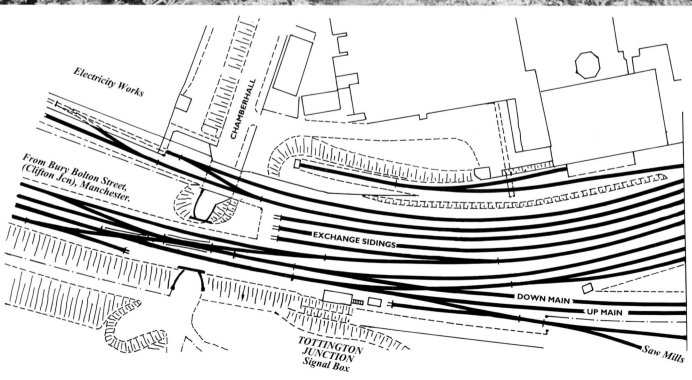

Electricity Works

CHAMBERHALL

From Bury Bolton Street,
(Clifton Jcn), Manchester.

EXCHANGE SIDINGS

DOWN MAIN

UP MAIN

TOTTINGTON
JUNCTION
Signal Box

Saw Mills

Saturday morning (09.30) activity at Tottington Junction, 22nd June 1963. Bury's own "Jinty", 0-6-0, **47584**, is busily engaged in a spot of shunting, drawing a small number of coal wagons off the Tottington Branch Sidings. The engine is about to pass over the brick arch which spanned Chamber Hall Street. Tottington Junction signal box was rarely photographed so we are fortunate in having this view showing the end and rear of the box. The all-timber structure was a relative newcomer on the scene, being a replacement box erected in 1923, some ten yards further south than its predecessor; it was subsequently closed on 25th September 1967. The original box had been opened to coincide with the opening of the Tottington Branch on 6th November 1882. No one can fail to notice Peel Mills chimney casting a dark presence over the proceedings. The Company which built these mills took its name from the family which brought prosperity to the town. No.1 Mill (1885-7) was reduced in height in 1963 (far left behind the ICI tank wagon); No.2 Mill (1892) can be seen behind the chimney; and No.3 Mill (1913-15) is out of sight. Peel Mills (Holdings) Ltd. took their water supply from the river Irwell close by. Note the bridge spanning the main line beyond the signal box. This originally connected Park Road to Arthur Ashworth's Chemical Works and has an interesting history. The superstructure was renewed and widened, and provided with an additional walkway in 1957, all resting on the original abutments which were strengthened with steel stanchions. Steel main girders and cross-girders replaced the original materials, and a concrete deck was added. The bridge continued to provide access to Messrs Walker Chemical Company during the 1960s. *Eric Bentley*

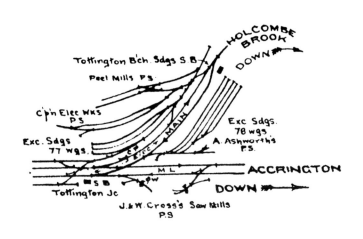

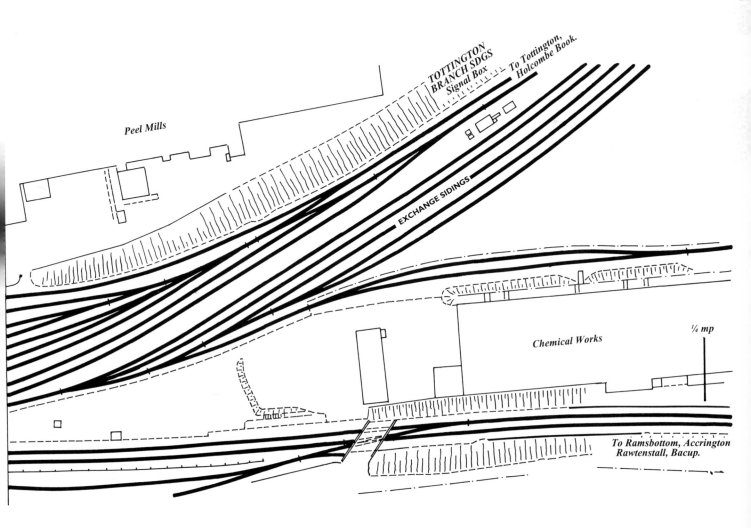

Bridge No.34, more commonly known locally as Calrow's Viaduct, was the first of two crossings of the Irwell at the location of Burrs, north of Bury. Bridge No.34 consisted of three metal spans of 44 feet which were supported on stone piers. The steel main girders and cross girders carried a concrete deck and was reconstructed in 1927. The twin-arched spans at both ends of the bridge had an 18feet skew span. In this photograph, we catch sight of a Cravens 2-car Dmu as it glides over the bridge on a Rawtenstall to Bury service, on the 8th April 1971.

Ray Farrell

At 10.25 on Saturday, 15th August 1964, we see the shallow embankment which stretched between bridge No.34, Calrow's Viaduct (two arches of which can be seen far right), and bridge No.35 (a glimpse of the metal span of which is just visible, far left). From the derelict ground left by an erstwhile glue factory which existed at Burrs, we see a Knowsley Street Station to Bacup pick-up freight passing along the embankment, hauled by a Crab. Visitors to this very spot today will find the area much more pleasant now that the "Burrs Countryside Heritage and Outdoor Pursuits Area" has been created. *Eric Bentley*

The picturesque part of Burrs lay adjacent bridge No 35, Burrs Viaduct, which was located at the northern end of the embankment. At both ends of the main metal span is a brick arch with stone abutments and piers. The arch on the northern, or Ramsbottom side, carried the railway over Hows Lane, a public right of way. Making progress towards Rams-bottom is a Blackpool Illuminations special from Knowsley Street, furnishing a half-day visit to the resort on Monday, 20th September 1965. The time is 12.50, and allowing for stops scheduled and unsched-uled, the train will arrive at its destination in the early afternoon, giving excursionists the time to take a stroll along the prom-enade, imbibe the sea air, and partake of an evening meal before enjoying the delights of the "lights". Black 5, **45258** (Bolton shed) heads the lengthy train towards Ramsbottom, the next stop on its journey.   *Eric Bentley*

Burrs Viaduct carries the Bury to Rams-bottom line over the northern arm of the deeply incised meander of the Irwell at this location. The substratum in the vicin-ity of Bury comprises a thick layer of boulder clay of glacial origin into which the river, over centuries, has eroded a deep channel. The main wrought iron bridge of 55 feet span resulted from renewal in 1877, later to be strengthened in 1896; the method for doing that can be seen in the girder set back beneath the upper ribbed span. The arches at either end were 25 feet 4 ins wide, the unmetalled Hows Lane making use of the way through the left-hand arch. A Cravens twin-car Dmu rum-bles across the bridge towards Rams-bottom on the 8th April 1971. *Ray Farrell*

(Left) With Holcombe Tower in the background, Black 5, **44868** (Stockport shed), approaches the foot crossing to the Brown Cow public house, north of Burrs with the 17.10 Nelson to Moston Sidings Class D freight, at 18.30, Tuesday, 30th July 1963. Apart from making a three-quarter study of the locomotive, highlighted by the evening sunlight, it is of interest to mention the difference in the permanent way at this location. The Up line is made up of bullhead rail, held in cast iron chairs by spring clips. Flat-bottom rails form the Down line, with steel pegs securing the rails to timber sleepers, much of which was re-laid during 1961. The structure adjacent to the Down line is a masonry pier which formerly supported a three span cast-iron arched overbridge that carried a track from Touch Road Farm into fields at Castle Steads, the site of a Roman Fort. *Eric Bentley*

From the top of Summerseat Cutting, amongst the foliage, we have an almost furtive glance down at the railway as Stanier, **42547** (Rose Grove shed) approaches Summerseat Station with the 16.20(Sx) Manchester Victoria to Colne service. The height of the stop signal is impressive, mounted at the top of a tubular post which itself is perched on the end of a right-hand bracket at the top of a steel broad flange beam post. The great height is a response to the need for a signal which can be clearly seen despite line curvature and obstruction such as Summerseat Station buildings. The time is at 16.50, on Monday, 23rd September 1964.

Eric Bentley

Summerseat

In a sunlit, sylvan setting, the passage is recorded of Black 5, No **45154**, *The Lanarkshire Yeomanry*, a Newton Heath engine, as it approaches Chest Wheel foot crossing south of Summerseat Station, at 18.18, Tuesday, 28th May 1963. The train formed the 17.10 Nelson to Moston Sidings van freight. The crossing, marked by the timber boarding laid longitudinally between the rails, just beyond the signal post, continued an old pedestrian route leading from Wood Road Lane, via Chest Wheel Bridge over the Irwell, and on to the eastern side of the railway. Following this footpath led the walker either northwards to Summerseat, or southwards towards Olive's Siding, and beyond. Careful study of the right-hand bracket signal will reveal a white diamond-shaped plate, half way up the signal post, this informed the train crew that their presence at the signal was indicated at the controlling signal box. This plate exempted the train crew from carrying out Rule 55 which stated that when a train was detained at a stop signal showing danger, the signalman must be reminded of its presence by one of the crew walking to the box to advise the signalman in person.
Eric Bentley

The 16.30 Bacup to Manchester Victoria train, in the form of a Metro Cammell two-car set, leaves bucolic Summerseat Station at 16.53, Monday, 23rd September 1963. The Upside station buildings were located at the Bury end of the low-level portion of the platform; the rise in the platform to the normal height can be clearly seen on this and other photographs. Raising of the platform at Summerseat took place in 1890, some years after a Board of Trade directive which applied to all railway companies. The main station building was 64 feet long, 24 feet wide, and measured 12 feet from the platform surface to the eaves. The building housed a booking office, booking hall, general waiting room, and a ladies' waiting room. Living accommodation was added to the building around 1890 and differed in style to the original. The earlier (1860) building was redolent of ELR design, with arched windows, dressed corner stones, and a platform awning integral with the hipped roof. The story of decline of the station makes an interesting account but it is sufficient here to note that approval for its demolition was given on the 28th October 1970, the work being completed by 26th March 1971; the station then lingered on until closure on 5th June 1972. In the final year, the Upside platform complemented that on the Down side in having a simple timber shelter.   *Eric Bentley*

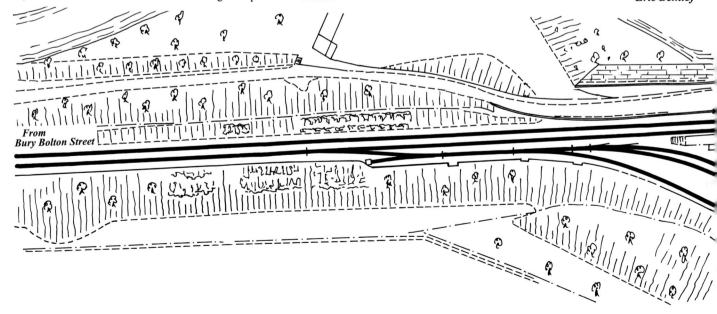

From
Bury Bolton Street

From elevated ground overlooking Summerseat Station and goods yard, "Crab" No. **42726** (Newton Heath shed) approaches the station with a day excursion to either Blackpool or Morecambe. Its journey will take the train via the main line from Stubbins Junction, Helmshore, Haslingden, Accrington, Blackburn, and to Preston. This Sunday excursion was photographed at 10.30 on the 23rd July 1961 and from this vantage point it is also possible to see the small timber waiting shelter on the Down platform - a design perpetuated on the East Lancashire Railway today. Five months have elapsed since a child was killed while crossing the lines on the barrow crossing at the base of the Down platform ramp. Note that there is as yet no footbridge. The gentle rise of Holcombe Hill forms an impressive background to the station at which this tragedy occurred, the monument to Sir Robert Peel standing at 1,000 feet above sea level.

Eric Bentley

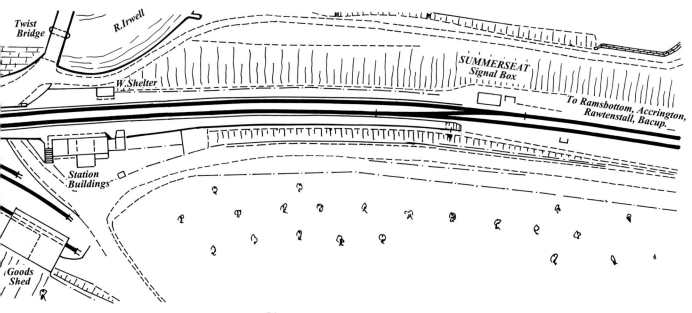

Summerseat

Entering Summerseat Cutting on a sunny Tuesday evening, 28th May 1963, is one of Bury's Fowler Midland 4F 0-6-0s, No **43880**, drawing the 16.45 Bacup to Moston Sidings Class D goods towards Bury. There were two running lines at this location, the Up Main, along which the goods train is running, and the Down Main. The third line, on the right, formed a short headshunt for the goods yard and finished a few yards further on. It was off this line that the three sidings could be entered or left, to and from the goods yard. To enter, it was necessary to set-back from the Up Main, the last vehicle of a train having to clear the points before setting-back. The connection between the Up sidings to the Up Main was removed in 1965. The small platform building to the right of the guard's van in the train was an oil store and lamp room.

A long way from home, 2-6-0 5MT, **42946** (Nuneaton shed), passes Summerseat with the 16.45 Bacup to Moston Sidings Class D van freight at 18.10, Thursday, 25th July 1963. It would be interesting to know the purpose of the trackside sign in front of the signal post. Just outside the entrance to the warehouse is the loading gauge; the majority of goods yards had one, and Summerseat was no exception, although use of the gauge by this date would be at an end. W.A.Stanier's 2-6-0s were the first main line engines for the LMS after his appointment to Chief Mechanical Engineer in 1932, and forty such locomotives were built and later fitted with superheaters. Unlike the Crabs, it was possible to mount the 18ins by 28ins cylinders horizontally, and with a working pressure of 225lbs/sq.in, have the engines equal in tractive effort as the Hughes' Crabs.

Eric Bentley (2)

(Above) **Summerseat Station** in the summer months of 1955 when the railway still enjoyed a distinctly manicured look about it, the days when lineside hedgerows and vegetation was controlled by locally based gangs of men. Note also the lack of fencing along the low level section of platform and the still to be erected footbridge.

C H A Townley, courtesy J A Peden

(Right) **An unidentified Black 5** sweeps round the curve and through Summerseat Station beneath the belated footbridge with the often photographed 17.10 Nelson to Moston Sidings freight, capturing it once again on film, this time at 18.20, 21st August 1964. In this view it is possible to see the stone retaining wall and parapet which formed bridge No.39 which spanned Railway Street. Two wagons have been shunted into the small Summerseat Goods Yard which occupied a confined space to the south of the station. The yard possessed a stone warehouse and three sidings: No 3, the eponymous "Warehouse Road" ran into the warehouse and out of the other end; the two other sidings being somewhat shorter; the wagons in the photograph are occupying No.1 siding. Attention was paid to the retention or otherwise of the goods facilities as early as September 1960, and at that time it was used by Messrs Yates Duxbury for the storage of pulp. An engine derailment on the points leading into the yard on 5th September 1963 rendered the "Warehouse Road" unusable. The last consignment of pulp was taken out on the 18th October 1963, leaving the warehouse empty. Further expenditure on the yard was denied, and closure took place on the 28th December 1964. A 25cwt whip crane (No 384) in the warehouse was immobilised, and the building passed into non-rail use and still exists today. *Eric Bentley*

An interesting view of Summerseat Station as seen from the road leading down the hill to Railway Street and to bridge No 39. BR Standard 4-6-0 4MT, **75041** (Springs Branch shed), hauls the short 17.10 Nelson/Burnley goods to Moston Sidings past the station, and the now-abandoned goods yard. Access to the Down platform could be made by using the lattice footbridge instead of the singularly dangerous crossing of the lines on the level. The bridge was erected as bridge No 39A on Sunday the 8th October 1961 as a BR response to a fatal accident involving a five year old child as it crossed the lines by way of the barrow crossing on the 28th February 1961. A report in the Bury Times, 1st March 1961, described the barrow crossing at Summerseat as one which was in daily use by school children. The young boy was on his way to school and was caught by the 08.23 Up Dmu train as he attempted to reach the Up platform. A similar accident had occurred at the station seven years before, killing a porter who was crossing the line in darkness. A recommendation by Ramsbottom UDC for BR to construct a subway instead of a footbridge was rejected on account of the expense. The footbridge was a stranger to the area having originally been bridge No. 247 on the former Great Central main line at Hollinwell and Annesley Halt, Nottinghamshire, which closed on 10th September 1962. *Eric Bentley*

CHEAPER HOLIDAY TRAVEL
BURY **9/6** BLACKPOOL

SECOND CLASS RETURN

Also to Lytham, Ansdell, St. Annes, Squires Gate for Holiday Camp, and Layton, at the same fare,
and from   STUBBINS, RAMSBOTTOM, SUMMERSEAT, RADCLIFFE Black Lane 9/6
WHITEFIELD direct or Via MANCHESTER 9/6
RADCLIFFE Central direct 9/6, Via MANCHESTER 10/6

By any train, any day from Friday 3rd July to Saturday 18th July.
Return by any train any day within sixteen days from date of issue of ticket. Not available for
break of journey or for alighting short of destination. (See later announcements for regulating
arrangements on Saturdays)

With the summer vegetation in rampant full growth, the intrepid photographer has ventured off the nearby Miller Street (yes, it is there!) which parallels the railway closely at this point. A Cravens Hydraulic Transmission 2-car Dmu has left Summerseat Station bound for Colne, forming the 18.18 ex Manchester Victoria service. These distinctive sets were introduced in 1959, easily recognisable by the two large windows in the front end. A further distinguishing feature was the large route indicator box above the windows. Having said that, they occasionally disgraced themselves, being prone to catching fire, in addition to having transmission problems. All those used on the East Lancashire lines were initially allocated to Accrington shed. Summerseat signal box is the focus of interest in this rural locality. The timber box was erected in 1922 on the Down side at the northern end of the platform, 85 yards north of an earlier LYR box (LYR 306) which opened in 1875 and was closed on the 18th September 1922. The box in the photograph was itself closed on the 9th April 1967. As signal boxes go, this one must have been arguably the most pleasant to work in on the entire line: bleak, perhaps, in winter; idyllic during the spring and summer months. Date of photograph: 1st August 1963.   *Eric Bentley*

The railway between Bury and Rawtenstall crosses the river Irwell nine times; this is one such crossing, the well-known Brooksbottom Viaduct. Black 5 **45318** (Bolton shed) has an easy load behind it making up the 17.15 Bacup to Rochdale parcels, photographed at 18.25, Tuesday, 29th August 1967. The chimney of Brooksbottom Mill, the base of which marks the position of the mill on the northern side of the river, projects skywards. Brooksbottom Viaduct (Bridge No.40), is located approximately 12 miles from Manchester. It consists of thirteen spans which are made up of ten 35feet span stone arches, and a 50feet steel girder span with steel cross girders and a concrete deck. The metal span was reconstructed in 1930, whilst arches 10 to 13 were strengthened in 1937; arches 1,2,3 and 4 were also strengthened two years later. Note the ancient two-arched road bridge which allows road traffic to cross the Irwell.

Eric Bentley

From the vantage point of a grassy slope on the northern side of Brooksbottoms, this panoramic view portrays the full extent of the west-facing aspect of the viaduct. Crossing it is the 16.20 Manchester Victoria to Colne stopping train, forming the 16.25 Salford to Colne express which ran non-stop from Salford to Accrington. The photograph was taken at 17.01 on a dull Monday, 10th August 1964. Note the absence of new housing in the village; the property developers had not begun to see the potential of Summerseat as a desirable residential area in the early 1960s. The population of Summerseat totalled 1,531 in 1961. Due to the location, the cottages have been built where suitable flat land was available. The small amount of flat land meant that buildings, such as the weaving sheds belonging to Hoyle's Mill had to make do, close to and underneath the railway arches.

Eric Bentley

On Sunday the 6th August 1961, Crab **42871** approaches the southern portal of Brooksbottom Tunnel (423 yards) with train number 1T65, an excursion to Blackpool via Accrington and Blackburn. The view is southwards towards Brooksbottom Viaduct, some of the east-facing piers of which are obscured by drifting smoke. The cottages in the right foreground, their fronts facing the railway, are stone built. The "Brick Houses", the front door to one of which appears beneath the signal sight board, were built in a somewhat cramped style considering the space available; they were built for the mill workers in 1885, an early example of social engineering by a philanthropic industrialist, although two features of railway interest include the tall timber post stop signal, the arm - in the "off" position - partly hidden by the reverse side of a sight-board. Such board presented a white face to the oncoming traffic so that the disposition of the signal arm was more easily seen. The other feature is the splayed configuration of rail on the Up line to the left of the engine. These were guard rails placed on viaduct and long bridges in such a manner to prevent derailed locomotives and/or rolling stock from leaving the "four-foot" by directing the derailed wheels within the compass of the running lines. The outer, curved guard rails were known by permanent way men as "butterflies". A similar arrangement existed at the southern end of the viaduct on the Down line. *Eric Bentley*

From an elevated position on the southern approach cutting to Brooksbottom Tunnel, we can appreciate the curved alignment of the viaduct which carries the railway across the Irwell Valley. At the far end of the viaduct, on the Up side, stands the second of the two goods sheds serving Summerseat. This one occupied a space at the head of a compact goods yard served by three sidings, one of which entered the goods shed. Access to the yard followed the same procedure as that at the goods yard adjacent to Summerseat Station. Observant readers will have noticed that the sight-board present in a previous photograph is absent, the metal bracket which supported it now supporting fresh air. At 17.54, Thursday, 23rd May 1963, the 17.11(Sx) Manchester Victoria to Bacup all-stations (via Middleton Junction) is about to enter Brooksbottom Tunnel, care of a set of Metro Cammell units; seven of these sets were allocated to the Bury - Bacup service in 1955. After several years of hard running they were said to ride poorly at speed owing to the "hunting" of the bogies. Such sets could be identified by the multiple-unit control jumper cable sockets which were placed at the front end on both sides. *Eric Bentley*

Another of Bury's Crabs, 42719, emerges from Brooksbottom Tunnel with the 16.45 Bacup to Moston Sidings Class D goods, at 18.10, Thursday, 23rd May 1963. From this trackside viewpoint, it can be appreciated why a sight-board was necessary behind the signal arm, for on dull days and in winter, it would have merged into the dark background formed by the tunnel masonry and the rising bank above, not to mention the sleeper fencing, which was ubiquitous throughout the railway system and was still a common feature as seen here, rising in a graceful curve up the bank and over the top of the tunnel portal. Repairs to the fence can be seen to have been made here and there, and a detailed look reveals that the sleepers were often cut into two lengths, shaped to form a stockade top end. Creosote and tar residue, a result of earlier impregnation, formed a deterrent to would-be climbers, particularly in warmer periods of weather.

Brooksbottom Tunnel and Nuttall Tunnel (115 yards) are separated by a length of open track in a cutting some 140 yards in length. This unusual photograph records for us an 0-6-0 **43880** of Bury shed, hauling the 16.45 Bacup to Moston Sidings goods past the photographer at 18.05, Friday, 31st May 1963. By the side of the Up line is a small permanent way hut, complete with chimney stack and a wooden door; such lineside structures were to be found on railways, main and branch, everywhere. A few still exist, but invariably in a derelict state. On the Down line, in front of the southern portal of Nuttall Tunnel, was a set of catch points intended to derail any rolling stock which had become detached from the body of a train; at this location, the ascending gradient was 1 in 132. Note the triangular catch point marker post alongside. The square-based stone chimney was associated with the nearby Nuttall Mill, long since demolished, leaving only the chimney as a monument to its existence. Nuttall Tunnel was bored to accord with the wishes of John Grant who desired an unrestricted view across the valley from his home at Nuttall Hall Farm. *Eric Bentley(2)*

Nine tall chimneys mark the location of the town of Ramsbottom as seen from above the castellated and turreted north-facing portal of Nuttall Tunnel. The reason for the embellishments were to concur with the wishes of John Grant who had demanded a tunnel, not just any old tunnel, but one which at either end had pretensions to look like a castle. At 13 miles from Clifton Junction, Jubilee **45622**, *Boscawen*, a Newton Heath engine, descends the gradient with the 17.10 Nelson to Moston Sidings goods, photographed at 18.20, Friday, 13th May 1963. A close-up of one of the masonry turrets appears on the left. What cannot be seen are two faces carved in the stone, and reputed to represent the faces of two of the East Lancashire Railway Company directors. Note the long length of sleeper fencing which borders the railway-owned property on the eastern side, the BR concrete, and L&Y timber mileposts in the foreground, and the distinctive striped distant signal post.

A view from the "battlements" at Nuttall Tunnel, the north portal. Crab **42700** approaches the tunnel in charge of the 16.45 Bacup to Moston Sidings goods, a regular evening study for the photographer, taken on this occasion at 18.08, Wednesday, 22nd May 1963. This particular service called at Waterfoot, above Rawtenstall, and spent three-quarters of an hour re-sorting the wagons so that the original Class F goods designation became Class D. From Waterfoot, the train ran without further pick-ups, stopping only at Knowsley Street to effect a crew change. Note the difference between the Up line bull-head rail, and the Down line flat-bottomed rail.   *Eric Bentley (2)*

Crab No.42712, has a clear road through Ramsbottom as she takes the evening Bacup to Moston Sidings vans past the restricted height platform starting signal. The photograph illustrates the former ELR warehouse, which stood at the southern end of the Down platform, on this date, looking somewhat unused and semi-derelict. The sign on the wall reads "NO ENGINE ALLOWED TO ENTER THE WAREHOUSE", and referred to a restriction observed to obviate the building being filled with smoke, and the danger of fire. Note also the warning plates attached to the wall on each side of the doorway indicating that there was limited clearance. The track to the warehouse is heavily overgrown as weeds sprout unmolested between the sleepers. To the east of the Up platform, Ramsbottom Station sidings contain a few vans. In their heyday, these sidings could accommodate up to 80 wagons. Modellers might take some interest in the concrete sectioned stone chipping bin at the lineside, appropriately adjacent to the rail joints. Like platelayers' huts, these receptacles were commonplace and found almost everywhere in great numbers and were constructed out of spare timber planking, sleepers, and later, pre-cast concrete units; this one is a mixture of both. The time and date of the photograph was 18.05, Thursday, 22nd August 1963. *Eric Bentley*

The southern approach to Ramsbottom station was photographed in 1963 from the uneven surface which formed the Down platform. In this year, the outward appearance of the station looked to be in excellent condition. The 1883 wooden footbridge which appears on many photographs taken in the 1950s has been replaced by a steel/reinforced concrete type of a much more lightweight appearance. This was removed on closure of the station, finding a new home near Hazel Grove on the Buxton branch, where it still stands. *G H Platt*

Standing at the southernmost end of Ramsbottom Station some forty years ago, it would have been possible to look to the right and observe the original ELR goods shed, and to the left, the compact goods yard which served the station, the town, and nearby industry. Entering the station roughly four decades ago is the 15.12 all-stations to Bacup train hauled by an Ivatt Class 4MT **46416**. Ramsbottom signal cabin's stop signal was mounted low on a post affixed to a right-hand bracket to furnish better sighting from the level crossing end of the station, a view obscured by two footbridges and the Up side platform canopy. As if to proclaim its age, an inveterate gas lamp standard has assumed a distinct lean towards the platform edge. Going west maybe? Reaching high is the brick chimney with a corbelled top, a monument marking the position of Square Works. The date is the 5th February 1955 when author, a young Jeffrey Wells, wore short trousers and was still at school, his free time spent devoted to train spotting, because it was the only thing that mattered; but not at Ramsbottom.

Photograph by ***Bernard Roberts,*** courtesy of ***J A Peden***

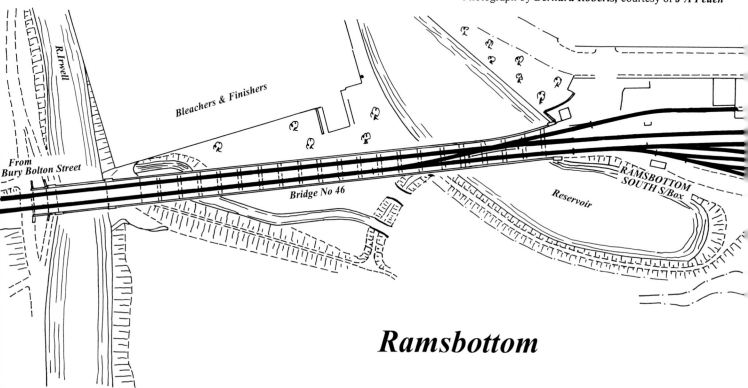

Ramsbottom

Ramsbottom station passed through a series of phases in which the L&Y added different styles of buildings over a period of fifty years. This is shown in the Up side buildings, one section of which is of timber construction of 1890s vintage. The lengthy platform canopy was supported by brackets attached to the wall, with a row of five columns supporting the same at the southern end where the buildings gave way to a blank stone retaining wall. Three styles of platform seats are also present on the platform, a choice seldom offered by present day train operators in place of the plastic surfaced and perforated three-in-a-row variety found at many stations.

G H Platt

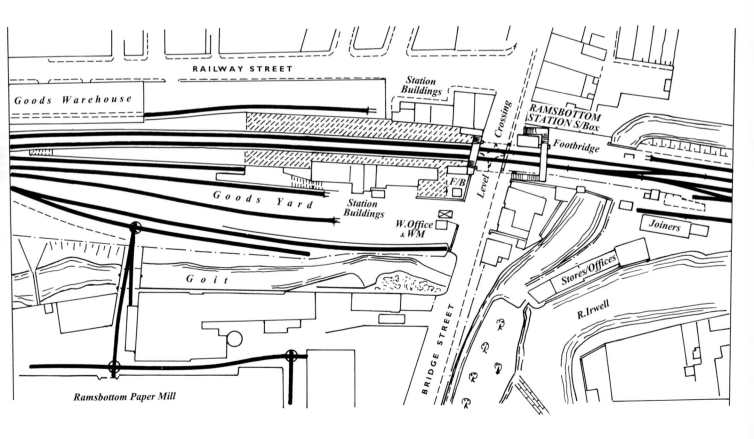

(Above) **Ramsbottom Station** was so typical of the rugged masonry built structures associated with the Lancashire and Yorkshire Railway. This view of the main entrance on the Down side, with its long wall behind the platform is what the public saw as it made its way from the town centre along Bridge Street. The large and potentially gloomy Booking Hall benefitted from the provision of a skylight, seen here at the top of the picture, to furnish natural illumination, and a small timber awning was offered as protection at the main entrance, an unpretentious concession to the public during inclement weather. To the right, and facing on to the goods yard, was a substantial curtain wall, which in fact supported the ridge and furrow canopy of the Down platform. When this photograph was taken, on the 5 July 1964, the goods yard and warehouse were out of use, the latter being demolished in December 1968. *LYR Society*

(Right-centre) **Ramsbottom Station train indicator.** Sandwiched between two slatted platform seats stands a relic of LYR station furniture in the form of a train indicator. This consisted of a wooden base, the top of which was slotted to accommodate a number of fingerpost indicators. Surmounting the box was an ornate timber upright to which a manually operated clock was fixed. Indications of trains due or about to leave were made by slotting in an appropriate finger into the upright post. Thus the setting shown indicates that *The Next Train will depart at,* the clock showing 6.57, this being a STOPPING TRAIN TO BACUP. P T L Rees, in his 1969 thesis on the East Lancashire Railway, states that an indicator was in use until 1966 for all Down trains at the station. The photograph was taken in 1963. *G H Platt*

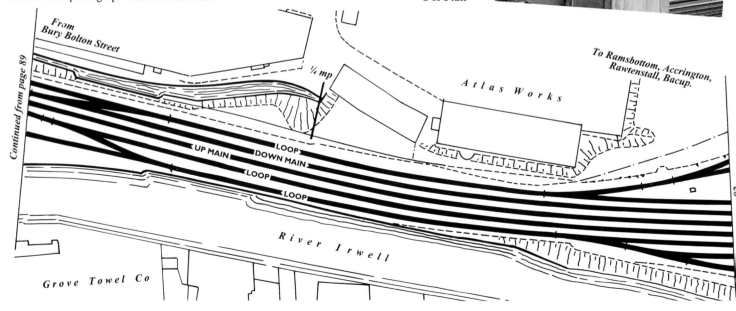

Continued from page 89

Bridges 47 and 48 spanned the lines at the northern end of Ramsbottom station. In this view both bridges form an interesting frame for the level crossing, the station signal box, and a Dmu leaving the station en route for Bacup. The sign indicating that PASSENGERS MUST CROSS THE LINE BY THE FOOTBRIDGE defies the temptation to cross the line by way of the level crossing - convenient, but dangerous.
G H Platt

Bearing reporting number 1T59, Black Five **44993** draws the 8.30am excursion to Llandudno during the days when large numbers of people still travelled by train on a day trip. The photograph, taken on 6 July 1963, shows well the disposition of the level crossing surface of timber boarding and the heavy gates closed to road traffic. Note the point rodding running parallel to the Down line - a sight now rarely seen on today's railways - and the two styles of lamp fixtures, the one on the footbridge being swan-necked, the other at the wicket gate a prosaic BR(LMR) concrete utility.

David Hampson

Stubbins

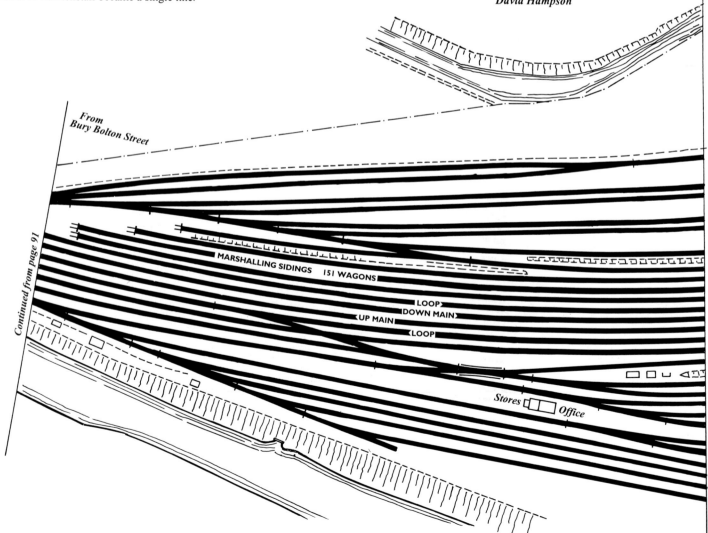

From the Up platform, we focus on "Austerity" 2-8-0 No **90408,** possibly on the morning Bury Knowsley Street to Haslingden trip, taking a light load on the main Down line on 4 July 1963. The signalman has pulled off for an Up train from the Accrington direction; note the off "peg" (signal) on the right-hand bracket just beyond Stubbins Junction signal box. The box was opened in 1900 as LYR 303, a brick and timber structure located on the Up side of the Clifton to Accrington line, at the north end of the Ramsbottom Marshalling Sidings and close to the junction for the Bacup (Rawtenstall) branch. The box was taken out of use on 4 December 1966, this date coinciding with the closure of the line to Accrington. However, official closure of the box did not occur until 17 April 1968, the junction ceasing to exist when the branch to Rawtenstall became a single line.

David Hampson

From
Bury Bolton Street

Continued from page 91

MARSHALLING SIDINGS   151 WAGONS

LOOP
DOWN MAIN
UP MAIN
LOOP

Stores   Office

Jubilee Class 45635, *Tobago*, makes a stirring sight as it passes Stubbins Junction with the 9.10am Bury Bolton Street eight-coach excursion (reporting number 1X20) on 6 July 1963. This is the start of a five mile climb, initially through Helmshore and Haslingden, towards the summit at Baxenden (771ft) which climaxes at a 1 in 68 gradient. The subsequent descent of the daunting "Baxenden bank" to Accrington, almost three miles with one section at 1 in 38, will almost certainly place an equally stern test on the engine and crew. A comparatively rare view of the Up side station buildings had been caught by the camera, showing the low-level flagged platform visibly lower than the present day running lines. This too was fenced off for the protection of passengers, in a similar manner to that at Summerseat station.

David Hampson

STUBBINS LANE

WM Store Coal

Coal Yard

YARD 208 WAGONS

To Ramsbottom, Accrington, Rawtenstall, Bacup.

LOOP
DOWN MAIN
UP MAIN
LOOP
LOOP

River Irwell

MARSHALLING SIDINGS 417 WAGONS

Continued on page 94

Stanier 2-6-4T 42640 has almost reached the junction with the train forming the 9.10am (Sx) Colne to Manchester service on 4 July 1963. At this location both lines are virtually on the level, the branch to Rawtenstall then rising at 1 in 132 and the main line rising on a gradient of 1 in 78. People who travelled on the Branch before the demise of the Accrington line speak of the illusion that their train was actually on a falling gradient towards Rawtenstall, an illusion enhanced by the ascent of the main line-referred to by railwaymen as the "Clog Iron"- towards Helmshore. In the distance is a plume of steam from Austerity 90408.
David Hampson

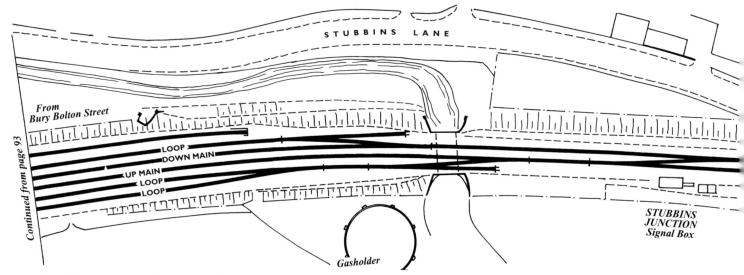

STUBBINS LANE

From Bury Bolton Street

Continued from page 93

LOOP
DOWN MAIN
UP MAIN
LOOP
LOOP

STUBBINS JUNCTION Signal Box

Gasholder

(Left) The front of Stubbins station presented an austere appearance to the approaching rail traveller. An unmistakable sign of ELR influence is evident in the twin arch windows of the upper floor, whilst the lower floor made do with more prosaic stone window frames. The upper floor at the rail side of the building was at the original platform level making this the main public area devoted to waiting rooms, ticket office, etc., Countless boots and shoes have trudged up and down the flight of stone steps behind the wing wall of the bridge to reach the Up platform. ***LYR Society Collection***

The curving platforms of Stubbins station are seen to good effect in this view of 4 July 1963. The narrow nature of the Down platform complements its shorter length than the one on the Up side; for obvious safety reasons, the rear fencing of the platform backing on to the Down Accrington line extends beyond the ramp at the Ramsbottom end of the station. Access to the Down platform was via a subway at the Rawtenstall end, and careful study of the photograph shows a sign on each platform indicating the use of the subway. Stubbins station closed its doors to passengers on 5 June 1972.

David Hampson

Stubbins

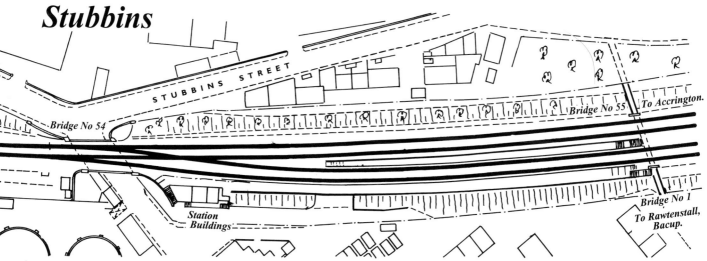

STUBBINS STREET

Bridge No 54

Bridge No 55   To Accrington.

Station Buildings

Bridge No 1
To Rawtenstall, Bacup.

Viewed from the shallow embankment that separated the diverging routes, well beyond the Down platform, this illustration shows Crab **42901** attacking the rising gradient out of Stubbins with the 9.40am Whitefield to Blackpool Central excursion (1T74). The date is 6 July 1963, marking another day in the procession of excursion trains serving Bury's annual summer holiday period. Away from the station, the main line resorts to flat-bottom rails laid on concrete sleepers and supported in a very neat bed of ballast - a credit to the permanent way men who looked after this stretch of line.

David Hampson

Helmshore

Taken from Helmshore Station footbridge (No.65), the view is northwards to Haslingden, photographed at 10.14, Sunday, 25th October 1959. Leaving the station is the 09.25 Manchester Victoria to Colne service, next stop Haslingden. The view allows us to appreciate the design of the Down side station building, much altered by the LYR in the 1880s but still redolent of the ELR, with arched windows and doorways. The flagstone platforms were a product of the LYR rebuilding programme, circa 1884, when the platforms were raised up to 2 feet 9 ins, five years before the Board of Trade made raising platforms on all railways compulsory. On the Up side stood a timber goods shed which was served by a single through road, accommodating a loading platform, and a 30cwt deck crane. There were three other sidings serving the generous goods yard, which in 1969, was described as derelict, covered in weeds, with no sign of the 7 ton capacity yard crane. An unusual feature of the layout was the single line siding connection (constructed in 1896) from the Down Siding and entering the fourth floor of Porritt's Woollen Mill by way of a timber bridge supported on brick piers. On the 5th December 1966, Helmshore Station closed its doors to passengers; a bus service was substituted and operated by Haslingden, Rawtenstall, and Accrington Corporations, as well as by Ribble Motor Services Ltd.

Eric Bentley

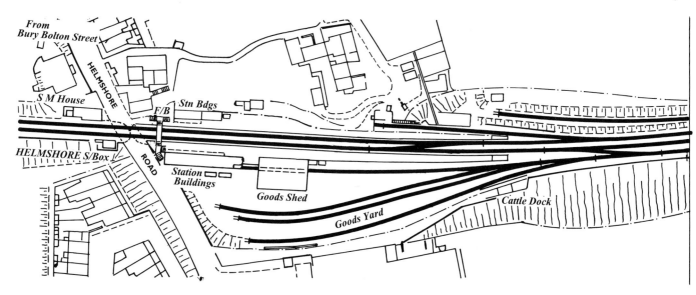

A thin layer of snow covers the ground on the last day of operation at Helmshore Station, Saturday, 3rd November 1966. A Cravens 2-car Dmu arrives at the Up platform, possibly on a Blackburn to Manchester Victoria service. Only a handful of people have turned up to await the arrival of the train, this being the measure of the use of the rail service by the mid-1960s. The timber goods shed looms up at the far end of the Up side station building, still in one piece and in the hands of a private owner. The adjacent firm of L. Whitaker & Sons Ltd retained the right of access to the goods yard which by 1964 had become, in railway parlance, "non-operational". A plan of the station and goods yard in April 1964 shows the sidings, crossover lines, slip connection to the goods yard, and the Down refuge siding redundant, leaving only the main running lines in operation.

Fred Collinge

The **unimpressive entrance** to the still-working booking office in 1966. On a wet and windy November day, two locals engage in conversation at the foot of the footbridge steps, while the dog on a lead waits patiently. The poster on the wall, between the door and window, advertises "Ireland - It is! Your Carways to the Perfect Holiday", plus a map depicting the variety of routes to Ireland from Stranraer, Fleetwood, Holyhead, and Fishguard. Careful observation will reveal the mirror attached on the far side of the level crossing, close to the front of the house; this provided the signalman in his box a view of the oncoming traffic in the down hill direction, an important consideration before closing the gates to road traffic. Perfect timing was essential! *Fred Collinge*

To Accrington.

Helmshore

The Up platform building at Helmshore Station in 1966. The single storey structure featured arched windows and doors associated with the design of John Shae Perring, the ELR's Chief Engineer. The building in view accommodated a ladies waiting room, general waiting room, ladies toilet, and the booking office which was positioned at level crossing end of the station. During the 1880s, the LYR created the general waiting room by filling in the open-air shelter which was one of the hallmarks of the ELR station layout. The extent of the infilled area can be detected in the photograph as the part of the building with the window boxes below the windows. The gate to the left of the wall-mounted gas lamp was made use of by railway personnel walking to and from the goods yard; hence the "NO EXIT" sign which is addressed to the public. The footbridge (No.65) consisted of a lightweight steel truss girders and staircase stringers, with reinforced concrete floor and steps. The bridge was a reconstruction of an earlier (1901) steel lattice girder type which had stone steps and timber flooring. The reconstruction occurred in 1938. Note the fire buckets hanging from the wall near the telegraph pole. The buckets contained sand and were usually receptacles for cigarette ends and paper litter. The line between Stubbins Junction and Accrington closed on 5th December 1966, the last train calling at the station two days before. *Fred Collinge*

Across the road from the station, situated on the Up side, stood Helmshore Station signal box. This was inspected and opened sometime during 1876 with a Saxby and Farmer lever frame and intelocking mechanism. In 1937/8, the locking room windows were sealed up as a bomb blast protection measure. Whether this was to protect the interlocking gear or provide a safe place for the signalman during an air raid is open to question; perhaps it served both purposes. In 1966, the box possessed 20 levers, about half of them in working order, plus a gate-wheel to operate the heavy wooden level crossing gates. The box occupied a confined space. There was much more space on the other side of the road near to the station master's house, and a position on the outside of the curve would also have improved visibility in both directions. Notice that the lower windows have been replaced by boarding on the rail side, leaving the southern aspect as built with glazing to floor level.

Fred Collinge

From an elevated position above the entrance to the 145 yards long Haslingden Tunnel, we have a stunning view of a double-header at work on the 1 in 100 climb to Haslingden Station. "Black 5" **44958** (Lostock Hall shed) pilots another member of the same class with train number 1M99, the 11.55 Yarmouth Vauxhall to Manchester Victoria service, extended to Colne. This photograph was taken at 19.25, on Saturday, 9th July 1966, summer evenings being a decided advantage for early evening camera work. The end of the train is about to clear Prinny Hill footbridge. Tor Hill (far right) looks much nearer than it actually is, as does Bull Hill looming up in the far distance. Similarly, the apparent curve in the line is much exaggerated as the map of the location shows the line to be almost straight; the illusion is due to the use of a telephoto lens on the camera which to distort distances. The only human being to be seen surveys his allotment, and disregards the passing of a train. In the not so distant future he would witness the passing away of the railway….. No trackbed remains; in its place is the course of the A56 trunk road. *Eric Bentley*

A Colne to Bournemouth holiday special approaches Haslingden station one Friday evening during the Bury annual holiday period. On arrival at Manchester Victoria, the train will probably form the 21.17 to Bournemouth West and will reach its destination at breakfast time the next day. Features of railway interest can be discerned by following the line of the train which has just passed Haslingden signal box. The Crab is nearing the hipped-roofed goods shed, and the earlier, smaller goods shed, both of which mark the position of Haslingden goods yard. Haslingden station is barely visible; only the station roof and footbridge are identifiable. The portal of Haslingden Tunnel is almost obscured by the public footpath which led from the footbridge up to Bridge Street. Eagle-eyed readers will notice the stop signal in front of the tunnel with it's signal arm in an "off" position, and also the bracketed signal for the Down line which indicates a clear road. The contrast between the uneven built-up area (dominated by St James's Church) and the rural foreground is very striking.......A farmer is at work in his hayfield; a solitary cow grazes; peace reigns in Holden Vale, Haslingden. All captured on camera, 3 July 1964.

Eric Bentley

Haslingden

A serious moment for serious men comprising staff and friends posing on the Down platform at Haslingden Station, before the Great War. The variety of uniforms reflected the grade or status of each employee although cloth caps and suits seem to be acceptable apparel for those off-duty. The view south encompasses the western side of the wrought iron lattice footbridge, complete with outriggers and overhead bracings, both of which lend strength to the structure. The bridge was erected by the LYR in 1895, serving its time until removal in 1966. Beyond is a glimpse of the northern portal of the 146 yards long Haslingden Tunnel. Note the sight-board behind the lower quadrant Up stop signal, and the two gas lamps close to the footbridge steps.

Photo *courtesy of the ELRCo*

The mill village of Irwell Vale comprised a collection of cottages essentially owing their origin to the existence of the Irwell Vale Cotton Mill. The village is set on the west bank of the Irwell where the river Ogden forms a confluence with it. The settlement pre-dates the railway, assuming a location where Hardsough Road, an old pack horse route from Edenfield, descended the hill side and crossed the Irwell at one of the few crossings made north of Ramsbottom. When the railway came, the village found itself with the main line to Accrington on its western flank, and the so-called branch line to Rawtenstall and Bacup almost running through it. The LYR deemed it expedient to erect a signal box (No.357), opening in 1878, on the Down side, south of the level crossing. The box originally housed a Saxby and Farmer lever frame, this being replaced on the 24th October 1924 with an LYR 18 lever frame. In this photograph, taken in 1957, the box looked in good condition, its four locking-room windows sealed up (as we have seen elsewhere) as an anti-bomb blast measure. The relatively unimportant Hardsough Road level crossing was made of timber boards, sufficient strong and durable for the amount of road traffic passing across them. Note the wicket gate; such gates were often electrically locked by the signalman from within his box to prevent pedestrians sneaking through on the last minute as a train approached. The box closed on the 19th April 1970. Closest to the gate is the Down Siding, and next to it the shiny Down Main line. Behind the box was a siding loop, and three short sidings.   *Tom Wray*

Ewood Bridge

Barely recognisable from Blackburn Road, Ewood Bridge and Edenfield hid much from the passing road traveller whom could be forgiven for not giving it a second glance. This was, however, the main entrance to the station, the building in view serving as the booking office through which the Up platform was reached by descending a flight of stairs. Date: c 1959.
LYR Society Collection

Views of Ewood Bridge station from the western end, and from the front of a travelling Dmu are rare. This unusual photograph captured an aspect reserved for those travelling behind the driver of the Dmu, an attraction which made the units so popular when they were first introduced. Bridge No.8 carried Blackburn Road and was a stone skew arch of 28ft square span with a set of attractive curved wing walls to support the elevated ground on either side. The Up platform extended beneath the bridge for a short distance; in fact, this view illustrates the staggered nature of the platforms well. Advantage has been taken of the flat land to the rear of the Up platform on this side of the bridge for the erection of a lamp room, this consisting of a door, two windows, a brick flue, and a slated pitched roof. Note the lean-to permanent way hut against the wing wall on the Down side, a welcome refuge during winter months and on those summer days when the weather is inclement.   *P E Baughan*

The photographer stands on Blackburn Road bridge in order to obtain this scene at Ewood Bridge station, taking full advantage of a sunny 5th September in 1966. The view is towards Rawtenstall, the railway curving out of sight on the approach to Horncliffe Siding, south of Townsend Fold. On this date Ewood Bridge was still functioning as a BR station; it had just under six years to continue serving the local people. Far left is a glimpse of the timber goods shed, here standing isolated in a field which was once a small goods yard served by three sidings. The shed lingered on, slowly deteriorating, although it is still in existance today. Note the crossover road trailing back from the Up line beyond the barrow crossing, at this date severed from its connection with the yard sidings.
P E Baughan

Ewood Bridge signal box opened in 1878 as LY 356 at the foot of the Up platform ramp at the north end of the station. The existing brick base was of LYR origin, the timber upper being a replacement to an LNWR Type 5 design which was added in 1928. Steps leading to the operating floor were positioned on the north side of the box, the room housing an LY 16 lever frame. Modest equipment for a modest box which was closed on 22 July 1962. *LYR Society Collection*

Ewood Bridge

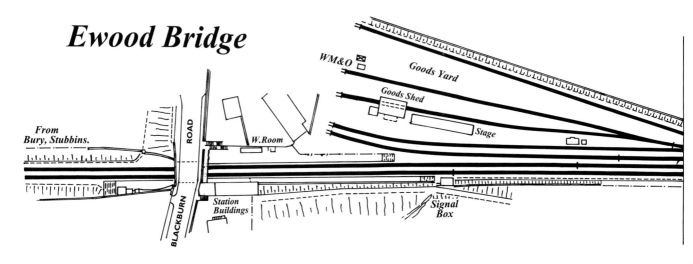

Everything Ewood Bridge had to offer can be seen in this 1953 view taken from the Down side platform in the direction of Stubbins Junction and Bury. In addition to the two/three-storey station building on the Up side, travellers' comfort was accommodated on the opposite platform by the lap board timber shelter, unusually, having little in common with traditional Lancashire and Yorkshire Railway practices. Compare this with the modern version shown on page 102. A well-tended rock garden graced the Up side immediately north of the lean-to urinals, whilst a somewhat unusual feature was the covered archway which formed the entrance/exit of the Down platform. P T L Rees, writing in 1969, stated that *"the windows are square, the stone work massive and well worked"*. This style, if anything, could be a copy of the L&Y wooden style in stone, even providing accommodation for the station master in the station buildings". The platform "furniture", in the form of seating, contains - on the Up side - two examples of Horwich skills, whilst that on the Down side was of pattern originally marketed by the Derby firm of Handyside, and which appeared in varying quantities throughout Britain's railway network. It was later made under licence by the LMS at Wolverton.   *Authors collection*

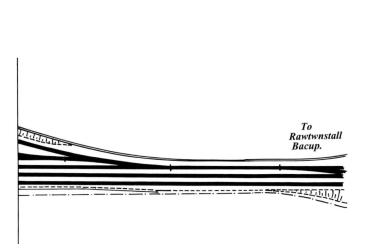

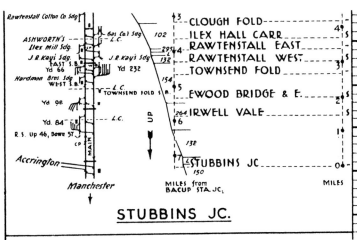

Townsend Fold

Even in the countryside in this small part of the world, there was always the mill chimney with its associated mill next to it. The location for this view as just north of Townsend Fold, a settlement similar in kind to Irwell Vale. At this point, Holme Lane made one of the few crossings of the Irwell north of Ramsbottom, and then entered the village by way of level crossing, controlled by a signal box of the same name. Ivatt 2-6-0 46406 approaches the level crossing on the Up line with a van and guard's van, past the caution signal. The chimney alluded to above belong to Holme Mill.

Photograph by *Bill Reid*

The view to the west from New Hall Hey level crossing shows that the Down to Up line cross-over was positioned on bridge No 14, the final crossing of the river Irwell made by the railway before reaching Rawtenstall. Records reveal that an original wrought iron girder and timber deck bridge with a cast iron parapet had been erected by the LYR, this required strengthening in 1880. Further strengthening took place in 1930, and a renewal of the timber decking and flange-plates in 1937. The bridge depicted in this photograph has been fitted with a tubular steel handrail held in position by steel uprights. The stone arched bridge in the distance (No.13 - known as Hardman's) consisted of a single span of 28ft which carried a footpath from the Burnley Road down hill towards the river. *B R (LMR)*

From a position in the "six-foot", but from the confines of the level crossing, the photographer has shown that the crossing surface at New Hall Hey was made up of a layer of timber beams - probably recovered sleepers - forming a road surface laid obliquely across the lines so that the heavy-duty gates are off-set to each other. Rawtenstall West signal box was a brick and timber/slated roof structure opened as LY 354 in 1878. The box was closed in December 1957 to make way for a new structure which was sited nine yards further to the east of the earlier box. Leaving the Down line at trailing points is a well-used cross-over to the Up line, whilst beyond the level crossing, and running back from a set of trailing points on the Up line, was the line into Rawtenstall goods sidings. *British Railways (LMR)*

South of Rawtenstall station lay New Hall Hey level crossing, which fell under the control of Rawtenstall West signal box. A level crossing at this location was necessary for road vehicles along New Hall Hey Road to gain access to two textile mills of the same name. Those on foot could by-pass the crossing (this had restricted opening times anyway) by taking New Hall Road subway which was spanned by bridge No 15. The short route merely connected the two mills on either side of the railway. The steel girder/timber decked bridge had a span of 8 feet and had been renewed by the L&Y in 1895. When photographed on 27 July 1953 the bridge was due for further renewal and was subsequently carried out in 1954 using pre-cast concrete beams topped by a railing parapet. Apart from these changes, the view remained the same as the days when mill workers in clogs and shawls clattered beneath the railway to and from their places of work. *B R (LMR)*

The driver's eye view from the cab of a Dmu which is entering Rawtenstall station provides us with a scene denied to the public without trespassing on BR property. On 12th December 1964 the western approach has a doleful aspect even though the basic infrastructure is still present. Of interest is the parachute type water column (LYR Register No.22P) at the ramp end of the Up platform, the unusual position of the Up signals (for improved sighting), and the remains of the bay and cattle dock adjacent to the Up platform. The 1906 ground frame cabin needs the attention of someone with a hammer and nails to keep the rain out.

P E Baughan

On the 5th October 1953, 0-6-0 No **52239** runs tender first into Rawtenstall station with the Clough Fold "gas" train. The camera has caught the driver straightening his tie before his arrival in the "Scented City" which was blessed with the Rossendale Gas Works. The engine was originally LYR No.469 which began its working life on 6th July 1894. Withdrawal took place on 18th February 1956 - the year of the Suez Crisis and the Hungarian uprising. Immediately behind the engine are two oil-tar tanks; oil-tar was an important by-product of gas works which at that time produced town or coal gas. The remaining assortment of timber plank mineral wagons would have brought in supplies of coal for the gas works' retorts.

C R L Coles R A S Publishing

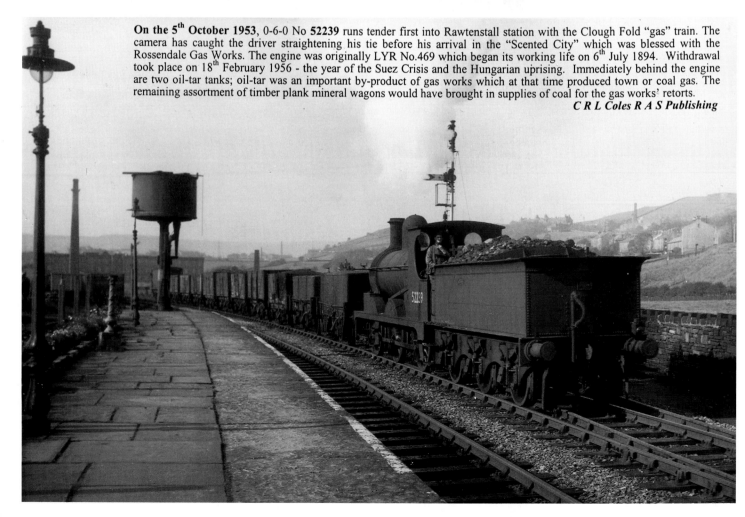

Rawtenstall station in its twilight years, the date being the 13th June 1964. The level crossing gates are closed to rail traffic, and the signals are on for the Down line. During what appears to be a quiet spell at the station we have time to linger and focus our attention on the infrastructure that comprised the town's railway amenity. Standing alone on the Down side is the Rawtenstall East Ground Frame, built like a miniature timber signal box, complete with ornamental barge boards and finials. Beyond the platform ramp is the ridge and furrow canopy supported on cast iron pillars, added to which, as though an afterthought, is a flat-roofed shelter with a deep valance. The main buildings were on the Up side, into which access could be made from the town centre. From the buildings projected an integral canopy, covering the platform where it mattered most. Note the flagstone surface, and the abandoned loading bay which has become overgrown with vegetation. A gents was conveniently located at the end of the main building, over the entrance to which was a bracketed gas lamp to illuminate its insalubrious presence. The platform gas lamps at the top of the ornate standards were probably out of use in 1964, the sole purpose of the posts by then being uprights to which the "hot dog" station signs could be fixed. *Author's Collection*

Ex-LYR Aspinall 0-6-0 No 52440 (Bacup shed) is about to depart from Rawtenstall with a Bacup to Bury Bolton Street service on 8th August 1952. This particular engine was built at Horwich and placed into traffic on 23 June 1906 as No. 247. Since those early days, the engine has witnessed many changes to the railway scene and by the time this photograph was taken, it had but a few months of active service left, the date of withdrawal falling on 4 February 1953, Coronation year. Along the Up platform we see the products of care and pride; whitewashed stones surround the flower beds whilst a shortened twisted or "barley sugar" shaped column has been mounted on a stone plinth by someone who knew its significance; and all is neat and tidy.

C R L Coles RAS Publishing

Platform trolleys stand at rest on the Up platform of Rawtenstall station beside the ELR style building. The position of the brass knob on the nearest door seems best suited to children or dwarfed adults rather than the average man or woman. Note, however, that in order to enter the room behind the door it was necessary to step down below the level of the platform. The reason for this would be due to the raising of the platform some time in the past. A fine suite of LYR vintage seating is available for those with a long time to wait for their train. The sleeper crossing laid between the rails enabled the station staff to commute between platforms, a procedure which was often left until the last minute and then done briskly, an activity which would not be tolerated today. *Eric Blakey/ LYRS Collection*

Rawtenstall

From beneath the canopy of the Up platform at Rawtenstall, the photographer's attention has focused on the Derby "Lightweight" 2-car DMU, vehicle numbers M79142 / M79684, standing at the Down side platform, en route to Bacup, on the 16th October 1962.   Photograph by *Bill Reid*

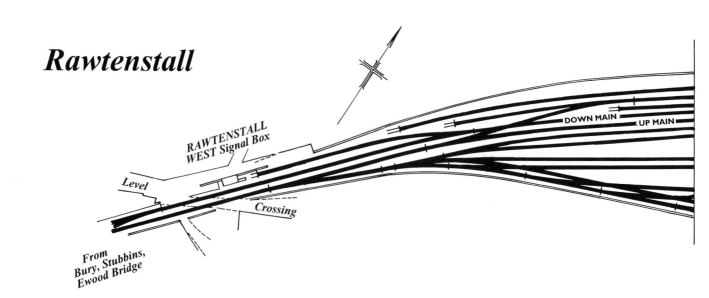

Rawtenstall

RAWTENSTALL WEST Signal Box

Level

Crossing

DOWN MAIN   UP MAIN

From Bury, Stubbins, Ewood Bridge

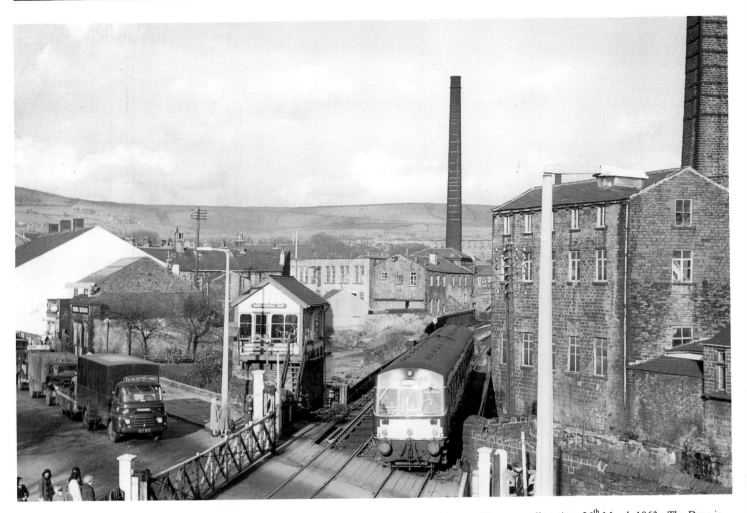

The 4.30 pm Bacup to Bury Bolton Street service glides across the level crossing to the east of Rawtenstall station, 26th March 1963. The Dmu is one of the original Metro Cammell units which were numbered in the 79xxx series. Rawtenstall East signal cabin was opened in 1880 as LYR 353. The top was renewed by the LMS in 1931 as type 11B to house a new 31 lever frame which was also fitted in the same year. The box closed on 4th December 1966. Road vehicles and a few people wait on Bury Road for the gates to reopen once the two-coach unit has cleared the level crossing and fully entered the station. The tall chimney dominating the background belonged to Longholme Shed, one of the cotton mills in the town, while the older square chimney on the far right belonged to Longholme Mill, originally a felt carpet manufactory which had its own railway siding.

Ian G Holt

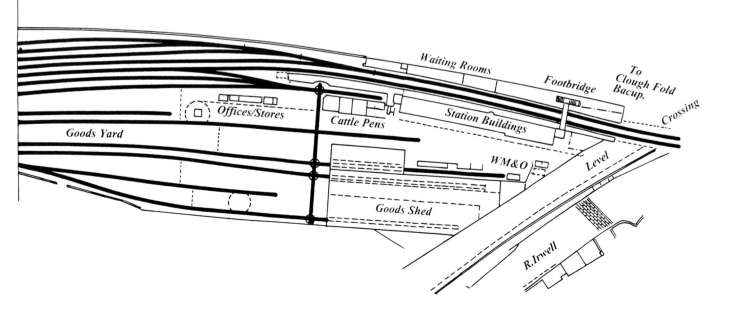

Rawtenstall East signal box was located on the Down side and occupied a space between Bury Road and the river Irwell. The timber decking and longitudinal timbers bearing the rails, and the low iron parapet on the Down side, mark the position of bridge 18. Viewed from the land adjacent to Longholme Mill, the scene on this occasion illustrates the gates closed to rail traffic, the signalman making his way back to his box. Through the Bacup end of the box there is a glimpse of the wooden desk on the lid on which is placed the train register book. In this the signalman enters a daily record of every bell code received and given, and the time of each train's passage through the block section. Attached to the end of the building is the toilet appendage with its distinctive roof. Not all signal boxes were given such provision, use then being made of station facilities or a chemical toilet. The photograph was taken on 13th June 1964.

Eric Blakey/LYRS Collection

Ex LYR radial tank engine 50829 (Bacup shed) leaves Rawtenstall station with the push-pull service to Bacup on 5th October 1953. LYR No.192 was introduced into traffic on 9th November 1898, the old-timer reaching the age of almost sixty years before being withdrawn in April 1958. The train is passing a small footbridge over the river Irwell which at this point manages to squeeze between the railway and the south-facing wall of an extension to the adjacent mill. This extension overlapped the river which was culverted beneath. Note the slate cladding on the gable end of the terraced houses along Parramatta Street - a common feature on buildings in many parts of Lancashire.   *C R L Coles R A S Publishing*

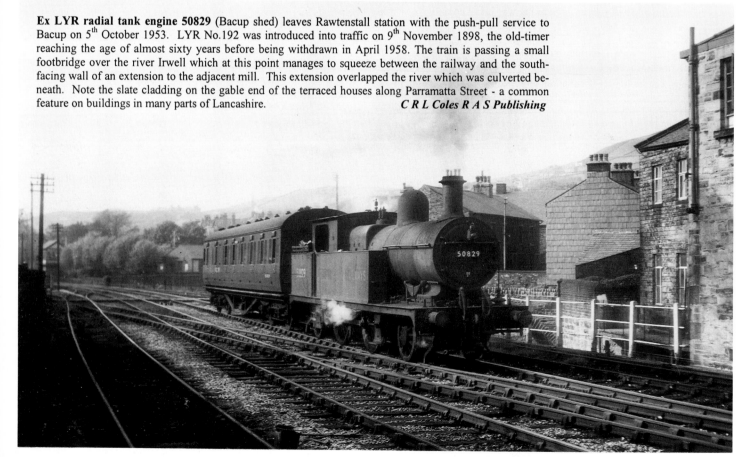

A stranger to this part of the world! Ex-works from Horwich, Stanier 3MT 2-6-2 **40091** (Abergavenny; Tredegar shed), in immaculate condition, draws a three-coach local train towards Rawtenstall station on 5th October 1953. Lining the railway on the left is the south-facing wall of Longholme Shed (mill) and beyond is the octagonal chimney looming over Ilex Mill which dominated the area around Fall Barn. In the distance is Ilex Hall Carr signal box which stood with its rear supported on cast iron columns bedded in the river, and the lattice trestle footbridge which spanned the level crossing at Fall Barn. The working was a turn carried out by Bolton engine crews, their turn of duty commencing at approximately 8.30am. After a twenty minute walk to Bolton (Trinity Street) Station, they relieved a set of men in the Bay platform. In the 1940's and early 1950's, the engine would be a 2-4-2 tank. The first stage was the 9.10 to Bacup and was first stop Bury Bolton Street via Bradley Fold East and Ainsworth Road Halt before travelling over the "Leckie" line. After that, it was all stations to Bacup. The return working followed a path via Bury Bolton Street to Knowsley Street, before continuing through Broadfield and Heywood to join the Normanton line at Castleton. Passing Moston to Manchester Victoria would see the men into the final leg of their "day", a working via Salford to Bolton, arrival being around 2/35pm.

Ex-LYR 0-6-0 **52549** (Bacup shed) with brake van in tow, heads towards Rawtenstall and is about to pass over Fall Barn bridge (spanning the Irwell) and beneath the footbridge at Ilex Hall Carr level crossing. The engine began life as LYR No. 239 and was completed at Horwich on 15th June 1912; it was withdrawn on 6 November 1954. The whitewashed wall of Albion Mill overlooked the scene, its position allowing sufficient space for a single siding to serve Ilex Mill. This can be seen leading off to the left. The curved terrace of houses on the right was named Alma Cottages; the terrace flanked Fall Barn Road, a minor highway between Rawtenstall and Clough Fold.
Both: *C R L Coles R A S Publishing*

Shorn of platform lighting, and the rails which once served platform No 1 bay, Bolton Street Station hosts the final passenger train to run between Manchester Victoria and Rawtenstall, via Castleton and Heywood. Here we see the tail-end of the "Rossendale Farewell" train comprising a mix of diesel multiple units. Nearest the camera is a pair of Cravens class 105 units with a class 104 intermediate trailer car; a three-car set of Birmingham RCW class 104 units forms the forward end of the train. The sets were provided by Newton Heath depot. The tour began at Manchester Victoria, departing at 11.05, arriving at Bury Bolton Street at 12.02 where a lengthy stop allowed the passengers to avail themselves of a guided tour of the station, plus a tour of the Transport Musuem where there was to be "an engine in steam", and the opportunity to see two new acquisitions, namely, "Warship" and "Western" class locomotives. The fare for the whole tour from Manchester was 30 pence for adults and 15 pence for children. The photograph was taken at 13.10 on 14th February 1981, two minutes before the official departure time for Rawtenstall, timed to arrive there at 13.45 where the train reversed and departed at 13.55. Note the temporary car park on the site of the ELR headquarters, and the vegetation which has taken root in the old bay and along the paved platform.

At 14.50, on the same day, the "Rossendale Farewell" tour draws to a close as the special crosses the ephemeral flat crossing of the new portion of lines which terminated at the Interchange Station. (The flat crossing was actually taken out on the 7th September 1983). The special will now convey enthusiasts back to Manchester Victoria by the same route by which it came. The steepness of the East Fork from Bolton Street is clearly seen when comparing the front of the train with the left-hand edge of the photograph. It is hard to believe that this site was the position of the former Knowsley Street Station. The new tracks in the foreground, complete with the guarded third rail, have been diverted from the erstwhile Bury Loop line which originally continued to the right, behind the cameraman, to join the Bolton to Rochdale line at Loop Junction. No signals controlled the flat crossing, operations at which were effected by telephone to the new Hagside signal box (opened 16/17th March 1980), although colour light signals operated at the Interchange station.

Both: *Eric Bentley*